Rocking Horse:
A Personal Biography
of Betty Hutton

By Gene Arceri

Published in the USA by:
BearManor Media
P O Box 71426
Albany, Georgia 31708
www.bearmanormedia.com

ISBN 1-59393-321-5

Printed in the United States of America.

Book and cover design by Darlene Swanson of Van-garde Imagery, Inc.

Acknowledgments

The heart and soul of this book belongs to one only,....Betty Hutton, who never before or after revealed herself so uncompromisingly. The force behind the mythical ROCKING HORSE that gave it it's last ride are Betty's loyal loving fans: the indominatible George Moffatt,...artist Edmund Arredondo,...Richard Tay of Sepia Records, U.K.,...and Lloyd K.Jessen, Editor of the International Betty Hutton Appreciation Society, among others; Jim Kason, without whose talent and imagination, it would have been inconceivable. To Laurie Harper for a lot of things and Ginger Sims whose nimble fingers put the text on the computer. The spirit of the book,... patience, encouragement and persistence belongs to Diana Adams. And the creative power who brought Rocking Horse to the goal post is Ben Ohmart, without whose faith in this project, it would have rode off into oblivion.

Dedicated to My Guardian Angel
Thomas Frances Cornelius Sticklmyer - (1927-2003)

Prologue

Somewhere in between her fall from grace - and God's will - in 1977 I met Betty Hutton. During the months that we spent together, Betty wanted me to know and understand her side of the story; behind the scandalous headlines of her life. Even the best and most intimate of the articles written had been unable, for lack of a close personal contact, to capture its subject. Not one of them could give an honest picture of the human being buried inside. She knew I had no desire to pass any moral judgment, as she spoke with me, about the flood of gossip. This is her story, her long hidden feelings; her heart – and soul.

During the time we spent together, she telephoned me every day and we usually met later that evening. Thus began a relationship which would lead me, and those I involved, into a drama one could not foresee.

Throughout, there was a trustful exchange. I arranged a reunion with Ginger Rogers. Betty introduced me to the mystery man in her life; the man she planned to marry. When their engagement was broken, she turned to me, unbelievably, and asked *me* to marry her! Yet to come was a series of events, in-conceivable at the start, as the story of her life unraveled. And because of this, Betty would be on the cover of the *National Enquirer*, read by millions, within the next several weeks.

Betty Hutton is not a broken relic of a dead era, gather-ing dust on a shelf. Her story charts the primrose path of so many young people of our time who have used drugs, alcohol and sex as a fast ticket to overnight fame and quicksand riches. However, best of all, it has a happy ending. A few months from her 66th birthday, a new Betty Hutton emerged as a college pro-fessor and active volunteer speaker on drug abuse in the New England area.

Her life and career could well have been a Faustian pact to win success. Many in her profession have compromised their soul to win it. She is the rare exception – reclaiming it before it was too late.

"ANNIE GET YOUR GUN"
An M-G-M Release
R62/102

To Jan
Loads of love
+ Luck in your
new venture

Introduction

Once upon a time, Hollywood lived within a glass playpen, inhabited by beauty and talent that grew older but never matured. Fate cast stones of time and world changes destroyed the daydreams and brought nightmares to its offspring left naked to the fans who, wishing to shield themselves from reality, wanted their idols immortal – forever young and beautiful.

The studio treasures were unlocked and sold and the nebulous stars screamed in the wilderness, reaching out for escape in drugs (Judy Garland), alcohol (William Holden), perversion (Rock Hudson), or, for some, the "Final Take," suicide (Marilyn Monroe). For Betty Hutton, the symbolic rocking horse ran away.

At age twenty-one, in 1942, Betty Hutton won instant stardom. She was earning $250,000 a year, pre-inflation. As if to make all of her dreams come true, she fell in love. Paramount Studios lined up top pictures for her opposite their biggest stars. Songs were especially written for her. One of them, "My Rocking Horse Ran Away," became so identified with her that whenever she appeared at an Army Camp, Navy base, Hollywood canteen or anywhere else, audiences demanded "Rocking Horse," and the way Betty sang it was as if she lifted it off the ground and gave it wings.

Ten years later the beautiful, painted, jeweled, shiny champion that rode her to fame and fortune was now rotting wood, mutilated, its paint peeling, its glass eyes blinded, its springs broken. It couldn't transport her anymore. It had reached a shadowy dead-end.

A sad, lonely end to a life that had once become so like a fairy tale, only to have itself played out in despair. It was, she believed, the end of everything; career, ambition, the material world.

Hers was a soul in darkness and when baptized by fire, reached out for help at the last desolate moment. Then, her spirit soared into the light—a light that led the way to a kindly priest and the patron saint of the lost.

"ANNIE GET YOUR GUN"
An M-G-M Release   R62/102

"ANNIE GET YOUR GUN"
An M-G-M Release

R62/102

"ANNIE GET YOUR GUN"
An M-G-M Release

R62/102

Chapter 1

It was a cold September afternoon in 1977 in Portsmouth, Rhode Island, when the telephone rang in the local parish house. One of the house workers, a small middle-aged blonde, vigorously scrubbing the kitchen floor, stopped for a moment then resumed work when the phone was answered by the church pastor. It was a long distance call from a theatrical producer. He revealed his plan to the priest as if he were a showbiz agent. During the lengthy conversation, the producer detailed his offer to send his domestic a round-trip ticket, with all expenses paid, to discuss the project. As the conversation ended, the priest put the receiver down, thought for a while, and then walked into the kitchen.

"How about a cup of coffee?" he asked.

The woman, singing at the sink, suddenly stopped, turned around and smiled at him. "What! Another cup for me to wash, huh?" she kidded. "Okay, Father, ya got it."

Father Maguire invited her to sit down with him at the kitchen table. He had something interesting to tell Betty Hutton.

Father Maguire explained the nature of the call. Producer Cliff Reed had telephoned to offer Betty a co-starring role with Hermione Baddeley in his new production of Noel Coward's *Fallen Angels* to open at the Golden Gate Theatre in San Francisco. He wanted her to fly out to Northern California that coming weekend to discuss it.

Betty looked up earnestly at the priest, controlling her inner excitement. "I like the title, *Fallen Angels*. That's me, all right!" she laughed.

"Maybe it was the mood of the moment," she later said, "'cause I said, you know, Father, maybe I'll take another crack at it. See if it's for me."

She had been the adored "Blonde Bombshell' during her Hollywood career from 1942 to 1952. When her career hit a wall, a series of financial and emotional disasters followed. She had been through four marriages – as many divorces and bankruptcy. When her last marriage ended in 1971, she dropped out of the public eye.

It was Father Peter J. Maguire, pastor of St. Anthony's Church in Newport, Rhode Island, who rescued Betty Hutton from despair by taking her into his rectory as a cook, cleaning woman and general housekeeper.

She got back in the headlines in 1974 when it was discovered that the former superstar was working at a Roman Catholic rectory, St. Anthony's. (St. Anthony himself had worked in the kitchen of a monastery in his time.)

Father Maguire could not have imagined what his charitable actions toward the desperate woman he would later know as *the* Betty Hutton would generate with the tabloids. Once it was discovered, they reported, *Blonde Bombshell Betty Hutton Starts New Life* at his rectory. Throughout this hectic period, her image as a troubled movie star engendered headlines such as this; always reminding readers of her past glories.

Spurred on by this notoriety, after a brief recuperative time, Betty took off for Hollywood in 1975 in an attempt at her first show-business comeback. She boasted to reporters, "I've had a facelift and I look fabulous. My figure is great. Nostalgia is in and I'm nostalgia No. 1." Apparently, it wasn't enough for the fallen star who had once been accustomed to quite a lot. She retreated back to her haven in Newport – and Father Maguire. Erroneous offers, nebulous plans and unfulfilled promises followed in her wake.

Just when it seemed that everything had at last settled down again, this call from Cliff Reed had come. Betty Hutton was going to give it another shot.

In San Francisco, a reception was held on Sunday afternoon at a Queen Anne Victorian House, called "The Mansion," on Sacramento Street in the expensive Pacific Heights area. It was at this point that I entered the "scenario." In the media, having had my own program on National Public Broadcasting, I was invited by the producer, looking for publicity, no doubt.

Tiny, seventy-one-year-old Hermione Baddeley, looking years younger, was very visible in the front parlor mingling with the guests and possible investors for the show. But, no sign of Betty Hutton. Gossip was that she had been drinking and after a brief appearance, had gone up to her room in a pique.

Within a short time, Betty reappeared, looking wonderful. There she was, at fifty-six, five-foot-four, trim, in a beige pantsuit, a full head of ash-blonde hair, long lashes fringed above her big brown eyes, with an impish look on her freckled face.

A decided chill came into the air. Hermione, surrounded by a coterie of young men, had been holding court, obviously being very amusing judging from the laughter heard. Now in no time at all, Baddeley made an exit, leaving a scattering of people behind.

Betty, bewildered, sat down in a straight-back chair at one side of the fireplace, rather lost and a bit nervous in the room full of gawkers. There was no noticeable sign of any alcoholic behavior. She seemed relieved when I asked to sit down by her.

"Remember, I didn't ask for this," she stated defensively. "This guy [Cliff Reed] calls up Father and asks for me!"

Immediately upon arriving in San Francisco, she was involuntarily enlisted as a celebrity fundraiser.

"I went to this party last night; there was this woman there who said if I signed up for the show she'd put up twenty-five grand. I wasn't supposed to do that – be at these backers' auditions. I was to come here to meet Hermione, the director and talk over the script. I mean, I'd never even seen the play. I read it though. I didn't know it was that old. So the first thing I said was it's gotta be updated."

Fifty years ago, on November 30, 1927, *Fallen Angels* opened at the 49th Street Theatre in New York. Its creator, Noel Coward, overall, was considered a "pretty talent," but a slight one. By 1930, he was the rage of London. He had had wonderful successes with *Vortex, Hay Fever, On With the Dance* and *Private Lives*; well on his way to becoming the ultra-sophisticated composer, director, actor and playwright – eventually knighted by the Queen in 1970.

Fallen Angels is a three-act play with a cast of six characters. The two leads are reasonably respectable married women, now bored after five years of wedlock, who find themselves thrown into a fluster over the arrival of a Frenchman whom they knew indiscreetly many years ago.

It was reviewed in 1927 as an artificial comedy, glib, with vicious competence, about the frailties of the human flesh. Although the work prided itself upon cleverness, most critics, and much of the audience, found it all tiresome – and boredom is the unpardonable sin in the theatre.

Nevertheless, there is some fun in the second act when the married ladies, awaiting their old flame, get drunk, let their hair down and, in essence, upstage each other. Probably for that reason, many actresses have taken the play on the road, in revivals over the years, including Hermione Baddeley in 1953 (with Hermione Gingold co-starring).

Fallen Angels subsequently failed again in 1956 on Broadway.

Now, affecting an ersatz British accent, Betty minced, "I could play Noel Coward – 'Dahling!' But, it would be a frightful bore. I mean, if I'm gonna come on prissy, the audience would be disappointed. It'd be a drag."

At the story conferences, Betty reiterated this point. "Who cares if it's done in London or over here – if you bring it up to date. You gotta Americanize the thing."

Baddeley, listening in horror, retorted, "Well, I hadn't thought of it as American!"

"Well, what the hell do you think I am?" replied Betty. "Now that doesn't mean I couldn't do it; but I'd feel phony."

It is no surprise that Coward was not Betty's cup of tea. Unfortunately, Noel Coward had died four years earlier and could not offer his opinions or suggestions.

One of Coward's contemporaries, W. Somerset Maugham, could well identify. Maugham had asked actress Ruth Gordon to see the revival of his play, *The Constant Wife* in Brighton, prior to a London opening in the spring of 1937. He was concerned with the performance of its star, Ruth Chatterton, a friend of Ruth Gordon's. He didn't know what to do about it. She went. She saw. Maugham asked, "Well?"

"Well," Ruth Gordon said, "I think Ruth Chatterton is fine. But I think your play has gotten old-fashioned and you should do something about it."

Maugham, who admired frankness, always liked Ruth Gordon after that. The revival ran for 36 performances in London.

Of course, once Hutton "rewrote" Coward, she then wanted to close the show with a few songs from her films, so as not to let her fans down. She would do: "I'm Just a Square in A Social Circle," "Murder He Says," "Rocking Horse," and some other favorites – and a few encores.

Now, in a near faint, Baddeley composed herself and in her best drawing-room manner exclaimed, "Really, this is *too* much."

As a character actress, on screen in England since 1928, the veteran performer was not about to allow *Angels* to become a star vehicle for Hutton alone. Not surprisingly, from then on things became progressively worse. Stalemated, the two actresses no longer spoke amicably to each other again.

True, Hutton was no drawing-room comedienne. She could transform a serious grandiose comedy just by silently walking across the stage. It requires someone smart and elegant to carry off that type of comedy, someone like Greer Garson who toured with the show. Like Nancy Walker, Hutton had a distaste for the lines. Logically, it seemed that she knew what she was talking about. She believed if she played it campy enough, looking frightfully upper-class, with a long cigarette holder, getting tangled in the telephone cord, shooting through the door (as the script required) and with the big hangover scene in the last act, she could, if she played it her way, make it work.

She had a point. People were curious about her after all the adverse publicity and her recent appearances on the Mike Douglas show and other TV programs. When they come to see Betty Hutton, and especially in San Francisco, where she would have a big "gay" following as the producer counted on, they wanted her madcap style.

Booked to open at the 903-seat Golden Gate Theatre before Thanksgiving, the producer and his associates finally decided to call the whole thing off. It had nothing to do with Hutton exclusively, but more with the realization that they couldn't raise the money: $101,247.00, to open for the eleven-week run with eight performances a week.

Actually, the show belonged in a much smaller house anyway. In the hands of dilettantes, none of whom had any production experience, the whole thing floundered and sank. Later, there was still talk of Vivian Blaine coming in as a replacement for Hutton but that fell through, too. *Fallen Angels* remained just that – for both the stars and the so-called showbiz angels who finance theatrical productions.

I was dyin' inside, Betty said. "Cause I knew I wasn't going to do it. Hermione didn't want me to begin with. I tried in spite of it, but I knew it wasn't gonna work for me. I wasn't under any obligation. I was only in for the weekend. It was all supposed to be so speculative anyway. But when I was presented to backers, that threw me.

"What amazed me most was that the producer hadn't even read the script. He was kind, though. He said he'd like to find another property for me; something more suitable."

Producer Reed called Hutton a "trooper," "cooperative" and indeed hoped to find something else for her special talents.

The story of the show's failure was sold to the *Midnight Globe*, a weekly supermarket scandal tabloid, by an alleged "fan" of Hutton's, a man who insidiously forces his parasitic attention on unsuspecting female movie stars, mostly passed their prime.

In the October 25, 1977 issue, Betty was blamed for the entire fiasco. The national article in bold type headlined "BETTY BLOWS HER LAST COMEBACK," misinforming its readers by quoting: "When she showed up for the first rehearsal, she had obviously been drinking to give herself courage. She blew almost every line and had to stop. It's a tragedy. She just couldn't handle another return to show business."

Down and out, stars are seen as fair game to any takers. It obviously was open season on the vulnerable Betty Hutton.

Betty was embarrassed and hurt and fairly humiliated by it all. Uneasy about returning to St. Anthony's immediately, she put aside her return airline ticket.

The last time she had been in San Francisco was in the spring of 1962. Betty Hutton took over the New York Palace with her own variety show and had a tremendous success, breaking records made there by Judy Garland. From there she took her show to the London Palladium, where she also broke records. She repeated her success throughout the British Provinces, before bringing it to San Francisco.

January 19, 1963, Betty opened for a limited engagement at the Curran Theatre on Geary Street off Union Square – BETTY HUTTON AND HER INTERNATIONAL REVUE – glittered in bright lights on the marquee outside the famous landmark. (The Curran was seen by millions of moviegoers in *All About Eve*. Particularly memorable was a scene in the lobby between Bette Davis, George Sanders and Marilyn Monroe.)

During the run of the show, Betty was the toast of the town, wildly adored by her full-house audiences, courted by hoteliers, restaurateurs, socialites, dignitaries. When the show moved on for its Pacific Northwest tour, Betty's successor was Katharine Cornell who followed her into the theatre on March 16 in W. Somerset Maugham's *The Constant Wife*. Betty left San Francisco in a blaze of glory. Being back now, it seemed like only yesterday.

Unfortunately, it was all a very different story now. With no money, looked upon by some people as a has-been who had lost out again on another chance at a comeback, Betty felt alone and stranded.

For the time being, however, she decided to stay on in San Francisco, ostensibly, for just a few days longer until she could get up enough confidence to face Father Maguire and the people back east.

Betty Hutton and Howard Keel discover that "falling in love is wonderful," from "Annie Get Your Gun."

Chapter Two

Marilyn Monroe – I met her when she first started. Johnny Hyde, the agent, was her big thing. Arthur Miller 'killed' her in my opinion. She had to be sexy, beautiful all the time. I mean we do get older and, damn it, the press would say she's lookin' kinda old. There are lines showing. What the hell do they expect? When you think of Marilyn Monroe, she was magnificent in everything she did.

"I knew Montgomery Clift when he was on the Paramount lot making *The Heiress* with Olivia de Havilland. I loved him. You couldn't help but love him. He tried so hard. He had a woman manager with him all the time. She was too much! Dominating, never letting him out of her sight. She should have been gotten rid of. He was a weak man but not on the screen. It's hard to explain that great talent. He was gay but I think it wasn't so much that as he was scared to death of women, starting with his mother. He was brought up scared: 'Don't do this' or 'Don't do that'; 'You've got to have the right friends,' 'Marry the right girl.' It was ridiculous!

"I don't think there is a happy movie star. I don't think it's a business you go into to be happy. Look at what happened to Judy [Garland], Hedy Lamarr and Rita Hayworth. As for me, I couldn't choose. I was hell bent for election on entertaining people. I adore the public. I haven't had any other love in my life except them. When the curtain went up, I could depend on their love – not that of the critics, not anyone.

"Goddard was smart. [Paulette Goddard, her co-worker at Paramount Pictures.] She got married to Erich Maria Remarque, went to France and gave it up right in time. She knew the studios were going down the tube and who and what was taking over. She quit while she was on top. She gave up a career for marriage.

"Marriage and a career – you cannot have both. I think Hepburn had a great time. She didn't have to get married. Tracy and she lived together. They had a ball. That's the perfect way to make the scene. You don't have to go domestic.

"The husband's feelings are forever hurt when you're a star. You walk in someplace and you hear, 'Oh, there's Betty Hutton' and that man hates you!

"Then there is *A Star is Born*; a classic story. Here is the man, a great star. He takes the girl – a little nothing. She becomes a bigger star. He gets plastered or gets gay. Something happens because you can't take the hurt. When you've given out from your guts all those years like I did, from the time I was three years old, it's rough when they turn on you. Not the public – no; what we call the inner circle, the power people, who control production, who cast parts. If I gave it up totally, I would die. Even at the church rectory, I entertained people – not singin' and dancin'. They came to me for advice – kids, married couples, because I have been through the mill and they felt I could help them; and I had nothing but love to give, then and now.

"I was going to be baptized a Catholic. I asked Father Maguire at St. Anthony's, please not to let it leak out to the press. He said, 'Oh, no Betty, just the Catholic newspaper.'

"Oh, no! I thought. I can't tell him not to. But I knew what would happen. Only twenty people were at my baptism, but the next day, Easter Sunday, the world arrived: CBS, ABC, NBC, UP, AP. And all of the European media came. There was nothing we could do. The press couldn't believe that Betty Hutton was cookin' for priests.

"I wanted that refuge of being with spiritual people. I arrived in Portsmouth after a near fatal suicide attempt, and dead broke. They were very good to me. They *are* very good to me. I'm not a big wheel anymore in the business, but the public remembers me. I still get fan mail. A lot of kids still think I'm Annie Oakley. I'm not gung-ho to fight. Once I used to be able to barrelhouse through because I had a mother then that I had to save. You know, my mother was tragically burned to death in her apartment. [Investigators reported that Mabel dropped a lighted cigarette on a couch and fell asleep.] I've never gotten over it. I lived for my mother. Among her things I found this envelope with 'Betty's Father'" written on it.

"The father of my sister Marion was not my father. I was a bastard child. I know who my father was – a great conductor and composer. I found out more about it when I discovered that yellowed envelope, but I always knew.

"Marion, my sister, is a beautiful, wonderful person today. My goal was reached. I don't really need as much – that curtain going up any more."

To people in the '80s, Betty Hutton seems more a reminder of the '40s and '50s, a souvenir of the times, recalling images, faces and voices of those long-gone places and things from the past: a pair of saddle shoes, a wide-cut grey flannel suit, 78rpm records, a black stand-up telephone, Dixie cup movie star covers, snapshots taken with a box Brownie camera, a faded copy of *Gone With The Wind*, yellowed newspaper clippings, a packet of V-mail letters, a service star that mother hung in the front window, ration stamps, an "I Like Ike" button, a military discharge certificate . . .

Historians maintain that great many events may tell us less about the past than the insignificant sentimental things accumulated by ordinary people, by those who loved them and could not bear to throw them away. If members of the swing generation had one unforgettable memory, it might provide insight into what they had been like, what they endured, what their dreams had been and which had been realized and which dashed.

Americans in the 1950s were caught between the atomic and space age, yearning for a tranquility at home to permit business as usual. Togetherness prevailed at home, where families listened to new hi-fi recordings, read bestsellers and watched television. However, they still left their living rooms for the local movie theatre. Generations weaned and raised on the celluloid dreams of Hollywood kept up their habitual movie-going. Periodicals reported the prosperous atmosphere of the 1950s, and every week *Time* magazine featured the world's most popular figures on its cover.

January 1950 began with Winston Churchill, and in succeeding weeks, Britain's T.S. Eliot, Spain's Pablo Picasso, Russian's

Malenkov, Italy's Gian Carlo Menotti, Siam's King Phumiphon and in the spring of that year, America's Betty Hutton with that exuberant smiling face.

Betty Hutton was starring in the biggest, costliest picture musical to date; the Broadway hit *Annie Get Your Gun*. At twenty-nine years old, Betty Hutton was a $260,000-a-year cine-musical star. Adjusted for inflation, that would be over a million dollars today. By 1950, after ten years in Hollywood, she had appeared in sixteen films and had become a top box-office attraction.

The most boisterous blonde of the movie musicals caterwauled through a number of routine jobs before getting her best song role in *Annie Get Your Gun*. This high point in her career, strangely enough, would be her last film of any consequence, with the exception of *The Greatest Show on Earth*.

Betty Hutton was not exceptionally pretty, nor was she a good singer or dancer, particularly by Hollywood standards. Rather, she had a vivid, firecracker personality. High-voltage showmanship and an earthy presence made up for whatever else she lacked. Her relentless determination to get to the top had flung her from speakeasies, to street singing, to bandstands, onto Broadway, exploding before the startled public eye – the frenzied high priestess of a nameless chaos, with music (wrongly named jitterbugging). She carried anything she did with riotous energy and an eagerness to please that she threatened to carry too far. She was a cross between the Furies and Little Orphan Annie. Her life could well have been an aborted American invention of one of Charles Dickens' characters. She herself admits, "I clawed my way up, through Vaudeville, nightclubs, movie show houses and contests into pictures."

TIME

THE WEEKLY NEWSMAGAZINE

BETTY HUTTON
The vibration was right for murder.

Chapter Three

B attle Creek, Michigan, a city of Calhoun County on the Kalamazoo River, bounded by the Great Lakes, is the trading headquarters of a rich agricultural and fruit-growing district and of densely populated Seventh-Day Adventists. Because of the Grand Trunk Railroad and the breakfast cereal food plants nearby, Betty Hutton said, "I was born by the railroad tracks between Postum and Kellogg."

The Twenties unleashed a new uninhibited spirit that created a revolution in American customs and behavior. In this social climate, Betty June Thornberg was born on February 26, 1921, at a time when American women kicked over the last traces of their Victorian ancestry. They bobbed their hair, dabbed on rouge, picked up a cigarette and took a drink in public. Their male counterparts of flaming youth carried a flask on their hip, wore a raccoon coat and spouted a vocabulary of wisecracks – all a veneer of sporty sophistication.

In 1918 the First World War had ended and, like most Americans weary of wartime strain, if for no other reason, Percy

Thornberg wed Mabel Lum. But the marriage proved anything but healing, serene and normal. After their first child Marion was born, March 10, 1920 in Little Rock, Arkansas, Mabel expected little from the marriage and seemingly got even less. Percy Thornberg caught the Twenties fever, quit his railroad brakeman job and loveless marriage, and drifted off to California with another woman, leaving Mabel the sole support of her two daughters, Marion, four, and Betty, two.

Mabel was the chief breadwinner for the three. As she would tell anyone, who would listen, that ever since her two girls held jam sessions in kindergarten she knew that they would do all right. A very straightforward and honest woman, she would tell you how she worked for fourteen years in the automobile industry as a trimmer, specializing in handiwork which involves finishing touches in interior upholstery. Part of those years was with the Oldsmobile company in Lansing, Michigan, while the majority of the years were with Chrysler in Detroit where the girls grew up.

When Prohibition brought with it speakeasies, bathtub gin, bootleggers and gangsters machine-gunning each other in broad daylight, Mabel decided to quite the upholstery division of the Ford automobile factory and open a small speakeasy. "Mom ran a bootlegging joint in Battle Creek and played the piano, guitar and ukulele by ear. I was about three years old when she taught me and my sister Marion how to sing and dance to entertain the customers. Mom didn't do anything real bad. How is a woman supposed to make a living with two kids when her husband has deserted her? We'd operate until the cops got wise. Then they'd move in and close us down and we'd move somewhere else."

Mabel then moved the family fifty miles to the capital city, Lansing. The little girls sang duets and while Marion actually sang better, Betty sang louder and with her rough-and-ready technique, threw in pratfalls and yells.

"We'd go around and I'd sing for pennies, nickels and dimes. We'd collect it with a hat and sometimes we'd go out with seven dollars."

"Betty was jealous of her sister right from the start," her mother said. "She was always in my lap, always after affection. She would stand on her head, do cartwheels, yell or do anything to attract attention away from her quieter sister. Marion was always good and helpful. But that Betty! If it wasn't one thing, it was another."

At the age of five Betty, caught in a neighborhood brawl, was thrown off the end of the pier, leaving her with a scar on her left cheek – a token which deepened her inborn inferiority complex.

Before long, the Federal authorities again caught up with Mabel's illegal homebrew business. "They caught my mom bootlegging. They took Mom, Marion and me to the city line in Detroit. I hated leaving school, even though no one was allowed to talk to me because of my background." She especially liked the school theatricals, where she could parody Mae West and other show business celebrities. She added that, what with living in a Lansing tenement and singing in beer halls (called gardens), anywhere they would listen, she had no desire to go back to Detroit. "I have no friends there. I had none when I was there."

Drinking during the Roaring Twenties became a sign of superior status for those who were able to afford the indulgence, or trade in it. Women who previously would never have ventured into a saloon now drank to show they were emancipated.

"My mother was an alcoholic. I would pick Mom up in bars. She often told me, "Honey, there's only two ways to lick poverty: be educated or have talent."

Unquestionably, Betty had talent. If she could no longer go to school, she would learn about show business by seeing movies with Vaudeville acts. It cost a nickel, the same as a loaf of bread, but it was worth it. She had not forgotten her first silent movie, *Ramona*, with Dolores del Rio and Warner Baxter, but it was the 1927 film she had seen with Al Jolson that had the most impact on her – a smaltzy half-silent, half-talkie *The Jazz Singer*. She couldn't sit still so her mother held her firmly on her lap as the six-year-old kept repeating she wanted to be a "tar" (she couldn't say star).

"I knew this was for me 'cause I loved to entertain people, too. I wasn't pretty but I knew I just had to be a star. Mom is the reason I became a success. She never beefed.

"I entered these on-stage contests between the movie shows where you get a buck if you won. They tied your hands behind your back and you had to eat pie and sing at the same time. There were about twenty kids in the contests and I sang 'Some of These Days.' I couldn't sing good but I could sing loud. I won every time. I had this great determination and faith. I went to Pentecostal church. I found God. I always felt my career zoomed after that."

With the stock market crash in October 1929, came panic and what President Hoover called "a Depression." It was getting tougher for the Thornberg clan to survive. Betty was now a scrawny, freckle-face nine-year-old tomboy.

"In those years it was rough makin' a living – believe me. So I sang on street corners and in beer halls. I sang with a mega-phone and I copied Ella Fitzgerald. I dug 'A Tisket A Tasket'; those were the songs I sang, along with the dirty parodies my mother taught me."

Meanwhile, pretty twelve-year-old Marion worked behind a soda fountain at Walgreen's drugstore in downtown Detroit for fifteen dollars a week and Mabel took more and more to drink.

Roughly two million Americans – over a quarter million of them between the ages of sixteen and twenty-one – were on the road that year. *Fortune* magazine called them the Depression's "wandering population." Mobility was in the American tradition. They had been fond of saying "Scuse our dust" and "Your Uncle Dudley's going places." New York drew countless seekers from surrounding states though the city had a million jobless men of its own. Most outsiders wound up on one of eighty-two breadlines.

"We're in the Money" sang the Warner Brothers films, *The Gold Diggers of 1933* and *42nd Street*, about an unknown girl, Ruby Keeler, who gets one break and becomes a Broadway star.

In the film, producer Warner Baxter gives understudy Ruby Keeler (Peggy Sawyer) the famous pep-talk backstage just before she goes on to face the opening night audience: "Sawyer, you listen to me, and you listen hard. Two hundred people, two hundred jobs, two hundred thousand dollars, five weeks of grind and blood and sweat depend upon you. It's the lives of all these people who've worked with you. You've got to go on, and you've got to give and give and give. They've got to like you. Got to. Do you understand? You can't fall down. You can't because your future's in it, my future and everything all of us have is staked on you. All right, now I'm through, but you keep your feet on the ground and your head on those shoulders of yours and go out, and Sawyer, you're going out a youngster but you've *got* to come back a STAR!"

There were times now that Mabel had to rely on local church charities to feed her daughters. Education was out for a while in her first year in high school. Betty quit at thirteen (having been double-promoted three times). "I was in a hurry to get out, to mind babies, cook and do housework during the day for a German family for five dollars a week. I had this great desire to save my mother and sister Marion, who had been drinking since she was nine years old."

Not long after singing with a high school band, directed by Harry Winegar, at a summer resort near Lansing and a year of touring Michigan and neighboring states, Betty, then fourteen, along with three band members, her mother ("who cooked a batch of chicken") and saved capital of $200 started the 676-mile trip from Lansing to New York in a ramshackle Ford. Object? Making it on Broadway.

"We thought we could set the world on fire. I managed to meet all the great music publishers as well as orchestra leader Tommy Dorsey. They all thought I was too young. They said, "You haven't got a prayer."

Broadway was harder to crack than they had anticipated. 42nd Street wasn't like in the movies where an unknown became a star overnight.

Betty told all the booking agents she was twenty-one. They didn't say they didn't believe her, they just didn't give her a job; advised her to go home – and she did just that.

One day in 1934, a dust cloud 1,000 miles wide swept from Midwest to the Atlantic Ocean, darkening coastal cities at midday. Cattle died by the tens of thousands. The inhabitants of the stricken farmland, bewildered by the catastrophe, began a mass migration into California in the largest numbers since the westward push after the Civil War.

Depressed people cheered themselves by seeing Shirley Temple and Jean Harlow in talking pictures and listening to *Amos 'n' Andy* on the radio. And, in 1935, the sound of the Thirties – swing music - was heard for the first time. Benny Goodman became the King of Swing overnight. In the decade that followed, there was some form of swing orchestra for every age group: Artie Shaw, Glenn Miller, Tommy Dorsey, Charlie Barnet and for the mature set, the sweet music of Guy Lombardo and, particularly, Vincent Lopez, who started the fine scenery and novelty electrical effects with his music, an earlier version of Lawrence Welk.

One night Marion's boyfriend took Betty to the Continental, a Detroit nightclub. The orchestra leader had seen Betty grow up and asked her to sing.

"The night I came back from New York I was singing in a local nightclub and Vincent Lopez heard me."

Lopez, who was then eating in the Lansing hotel dining room, was impressed and decided to gamble.

"The waiter came over and said, 'Vincent Lopez would like to see you.' 'Who's he?' I asked. I only knew from swing bands, the great society bands - who knew from *that*? But what the hell! He offered me a job and it was $65 a week. WOW! I said, 'Yes, but only if you take my mother and sister.' He promised to do that."

With the first advanced paycheck, the Thornbergs couldn't believe their good fortune. They took their first taxi ride, went to a good restaurant and ordered steak. Betty remembered ecstatically, "I had never seen a whole steak. We used to go to the markets where they threw out liver, innards – that was crap to eat – and scraps of filet mignon, that wasn't chic, that's not the best cut of the cow – and they threw it and we'd catch it in buckets, so we really ate well at times I guess, 'cause my mom would make stews. It was just that kind of life. I never had a whole steak before Lopez hired me. Then I had it for breakfast, lunch and dinner. 'Til this day, what do I say? Get me a steak! I gotta eat a steak."

About this time, Mabel heard news of Percy Thornberg after fifteen years. He had shot himself in a Los Angeles suburb and had left his two girls $100 each. This would make an indelible imprint on all of them, especially on the impressionable Betty.

In January 1938 Betty, at seventeen, began her job with the Lopez orchestra as a conventional-type singer trying to adapt to sweet swing. In fact, Betty didn't register as well as Lopez expected. He didn't say much, he just kept giving her another week's chance until finally, after a Philadelphia engagement, he decided to let his little singer go.

"When Lopez saw me [at the Lansing Hotel], I was in my own orbit, so I was really, ya' know, but I froze when I saw this huge theatre so I would stand there and sing very quietly, which was not my racket. I was so petrified and they [Lopez and the theatre management] were gettin' mad. That night Mike Druso, the trombone player, took me out to eat."

After ordering drinks, Druso began clumsily: "I don't know how to tell you this . . ."

"Tell me what, Mike?"

"Maybe you ought to have a drink first."

Betty nervously picked up the B&B (brandy and Benedictine) she'd ordered and gulped it down.

"Okay, I had the drink."

"You're going to be fired," Druso blurted out.

"Fired! Why?"

"Well, you know, the guys in the band never went for your . . . that kinda loud, explosive singing style of yours from the beginning. Now they like it even less, since you toned it down and, well, I thought you ought to know."

"I'm doing it their way. You know that's not me. Wait just a minute here ... Mike, call the waiter over, get me a double B&B."

That did it. She was "burned up." She felt like tearing things to pieces. She was in a reckless condition. And she had nothing to lose now.

"I never had a drink in my life like that and, WOW!" Betty said. "I went back to the theatre and tore it apart."

Between the choruses of "Dipsey Doodle," she began to throw her body around. She mugged, turned somersaults, hopped on musician's laps, pulled their hair and swung Lopez off his feet.

"I picked up Lopez during the 16 bars. Believe me, he was heavy. I swing him around. I put him down. I beat the mike. I stamped on it. I did everything."

Her voice hit every corner of the room from the stage. When the number ended, it was the audience who tore things up and nearly ripped the theatre apart. That was the night the Hutton style burst upon a relatively powerless world. Betty says, "I murdered the people."

Lopez was dumfounded at her whoop-and-holler technique. He asked her why she hadn't done this before and Betty could only answer, "I was frightened." The result was that Lopez signed her to a five-year contract and twenty percent of all her earnings from whatever media she worked in. On April 25, 1938, in Cook County, Illinois, she put her signature to a personal contract with Lopez. Although later she would regret this restrictive contract, Betty admitted that Lopez, ". . . took me outta the beer halls and taught me table manners and how to keep my voice down in restaurants. I used to scream all the time. He told me what to wear, too. He even changed my name."

"I picked that name outta the phone book, Betty Jane Darling. You wanna throw up?" Lopez consulted a numerologist and changed Betty Jane Darling to Betty Hutton and he developed a whole new style for his band to match hers.

During a Boston engagement of the Lopez group in the summer of 1938, rising band leader Glenn Miller caught a performance and was greatly impressed by Betty and her sister, who also sang with the band.

Miller, a trombonist and band leader in the big band "swing" era of the late '30s and early '40s, developed a blend of instrumental colors which became known as the "Glenn Miller Sound." Immensely successful, he died in a plane crash in 1944 while touring troop bases in Europe in World War II, but his popularity continues.

Miller decided to hire the more demure Marion as his band vocalist, reasoning she would be easier to manage than the more explosive Betty. She too, adopted the Hutton name. Marion was his star warbler until Miller went into military service and the band broke up.

The newly named Betty Hutton was a sensation and a successful tour followed. They then settled down to a 21-week engagement at Billy Rose's nightclub, the Casa Manana in New York.

Billy Rose, the pint-sized showman, once married to Fanny Brice among his other pursuits, was operating the biggest cabaret in the world. In the club he put on a spectacle called "The Big Show."

"I was just the band singer. In the Casa Manana show were these greats: Harry Richmond [the first performer who originated the tramp act, which later became a trademark for Judy Garland], Ella Logan, Blossom Seeley, Benny Fields and Helen Morgan. My God, the education I got just sitting there watching just floored me. You know, there is a showmanship in everything and I learned how to get on stage and get off. Take Eddie Leonard. He was eighty years old. He didn't do much on stage but he stopped the show cold. He worked in blackface. 'What the hell do you do? Makin' that exit,' I asked him. He said, 'Betty, I'll show you tonight.' And this precious man came down to my dressing room in his long underwear and showed me. He said, '... now, remember, when you start to shuffle off, look back at the audience, without saying it – 'Do you want more? Do you love me?' It must be in the eyes. Then the audiences can pick up on it. It can't be, 'I'm great, I'm marvelous.'

"It's gotta be that feelin'. So, I've always done him in my act and Helen Morgan I did on the piano. She came out with a white chiffon handkerchief and she would look up at the light and sing, 'He's just my Bill . . . ,' and, she really didn't do much either, she stopped the show. It was this magic about them that I had to learn and by the time I got going in the show at the Casa Manana, I had it down pat."

Backstage, opening night, Betty knelt down and prayed. "God, this is it. If I don't make it tonight, I'll never make it." The opening night juggling act didn't show up so Betty now was slated to open the show – to warm the folks up for the other acts. Everyone was busy eating, so she had to get their attention. Before she went on stage, she pleaded with the waiters, who had become buddies backstage while playing craps with her and her mother.

"Do me a favor, fellers. Don't serve while I'm on. I got no spotlight, no nuthin'. She went on without a spot. The waiters stood still with the crowd looking up at her, not knowing what to expect. Not a pin dropped. Then, suddenly, she burst out loud singing "A Tisket, A Tasket," "Dipsey Doodle," and one specialty number, "Old Man Mose Ain't Dead." The longer she was on, the bolder she got. She slammed the microphone, jumped onto the tables and, as she neared her song's end, inspiration came.

She rushed for the wings, grabbed the curtain and, using it as a rope, swung like Tarzan right off the stage, singing as she went. She literally stopped the show until veteran entertainer Lou Holtz came out and said to the audience, "Ladies and Gentlemen, you are seeing tonight what we call 'a star is born.'"

After the show, Billy Rose called all his entertainers together to talk over changes which the performances had shown to be necessary. To Betty he said, "Don't change anything young lady. There's only one thing I ask: Please don't tear down my nice new place."

The next day, she was the talk of Broadway. *Variety*, the

"showbiz" bible, described her caterwauling performance: "Miss Hutton is a petite and somewhat unusual type who puts great poundage into her singing, screwing her face up into poses at times that are very different and effective. She has a manner of working and diving into her work hard that finally gets under the skin; even if vocally she's far from the doors of the Met. Miss Hutton employs slightly wild, rowdy techniques that really sell her. 'A Tisket' and 'Old Man Mose' songs are right up her alley."

Now Betty confided to her mother that she dreamed of singing in big musical shows. Meanwhile, in 1939, Betty joined Lopez's group on a vaudeville circuit tour which played the east coast and Midwestern cities. With her rollicking style, she soon was billed as the first lady of swing music by powerful columnist Walter Winchell: "I can't explain what she does. Just call her America's No. 1 jitterbug."

Although it was an inaccurate tag that was to haunt her professionally for decades, Betty received an enormous amount of publicity because of it. *Life* magazine dedicated pages on the latest craze. The Jitterbug Queen herself illustrated to its readers just how to dance it to your favorite swing music. And jitterbugging became part of our vocabulary. About this phenomenon, Betty explained, "I couldn't dance a lick, ya' know, but I made a lot of movement outta my dress . . ."

The press capitalized on Betty's movements when Lopez was hit with a lawsuit. *Jitterbug Champion Defends "Discoverer" – Pretty Jitterbug Comes to Aid of "Discoverer"* whopped the headlines. Betty was front page news for the first time on July 30, 1939: "When cute blonde Betty Hutton, America's

Number One Jitterbug, swings it for a New York jury soon, it
will be to testify for her 'discoverer' Vincent Lopez, the sued,
and not sang, suave band maestro . . ."

The lawsuit was brought to court by Agnes V. Russell, the
wife of former G-Man Albert Russell, and charged that Lopez
"wasted and squandered on Betty the funds of Vincent Lopez
Enterprises." Russell, a stockholder and ex-treasurer of the
company, also charged that Lopez had persuaded Betty to
break her contract with the Lopez Enterprises and go under his
personal management after the corporation had spent thousands on "bettering" her talent and making her a success. Russell demanded an accounting and appointment of a receiver.

Betty, "the jitterbug's jitterbug because she can sing it and
swing it at the same time," was indignant at the charges. She
was quoted as saying, "I don't know anybody but Vincent Lopez
who is connected with the case.

"I am very grateful to him and deeply resent that anyone
else would claim credit for my success. He invested his own
money and time in helping me and I have never been under
contract to Lopez Enterprises. I signed a contract with Vincent
Lopez personally."

Attorney for Lopez, Bernard Thompson, said that he did
not think the Russells would have brought a lawsuit if Betty
had not been such a box office wow. Since the super-jitterbug
was cleaning up in personal appearances on tour, would sign a
movie contract that fall and had offers from several broadcasting stations, television and New York Hotels, this would amount
to a lot of money. The Russells had hoped to come in for a cut
of Betty's earnings. However, they lost the case, which was ulti-

mately dismissed. All the notoriety about Betty's jump from rags to riches was the answer to any jitterbug's dream.

Following on the heels of all the publicity, and always on the lookout for that next big break that would take her right to the top, Betty got a chance to be in a musical revue.

"I went to stock after I left Lopez. I did *The Greeks Had a Word For It*. If ever there was a play I shouldn't be in, that was it. But I did it my way. Libby Holman, Broadway's famous 'Moanin' Low' torch singer, was the star. Remember? She was the one who shot her husband and got away with it. For me, every night was like a new act. I was seen and from there, I was hired for *Two for the Show*."

"ANNIE GET YOUR GUN"
An M-G-M Release

R62/102

BETTY HUTTON, at the height
of her career in MGM's hit
film "Annie Get Your Gun."

Chapter Four

On February 8, 1940, at the Booth Theatre in New York, *Two for the Show*, with sketches by Josh Logan and the overall production supervised by John Murray Anderson, proved diverting to pre-World War II audiences. The cast included Eve Arden, Alfred Drake, Keenan Wynn and Betty Hutton, who got the most enthusiastic reviews. However, one review, written by the stuffy Burns Mantle, cautioned: "There is a riotous young person named Betty Hutton who has sung with the Vincent Lopez orchestra at the Casa Manana and in one or two nightclubs, who was the darling of last night's audience. Miss Hutton, Detroit born 19 years ago and as dynamic as the Harvest Moon Jitterbug, dances wildly, sings after a fashion, squints her eyes in a funny little grin, puffs out her cheeks and makes a lot of friends whenever she appears. She has a Little Miss Muffet number that brings things to a halt for a moment. It will pay her directors and Miss Hutton not to overdo her appearance. The physical strain is considerable and an overly stimulated vanity too, is bad for talented youngsters."

All the newspapers went wild with unequivocal praise, calling Betty "the real discovery of the year." Another critic wrote, "She was the most supercharged member of the cast," adding, "She looked like an adorable Easter chicken with a fluff of yellow hair."

Many years later when I was with her, 63-year-old Betty told me laughingly, "I did a song with Keenan Wynn, who played the spider, called Little Miss Muffet. I was in pantaloons – I looked just darling. I was the cat's pajamas . . ."

The show ran for 129 performances with Betty paying Lopez his twenty percent throughout. Then, when she refused to pay the bandleader anything more, he sued.

"Lopez wouldn't release me from my contact and he had me under contract for the rest of my life." Prevented from working, she took accommodating dates. "I played bar mitzvahs, weddings, you name it – and I got $65 bucks a week."

When Lopez brought about a breach-of-contract suit, Betty consulted the top theatrical lawyer of the day, Abe Berman. Betty paced up and down Berman's office shouting how unfair it all was. She hadn't worked in months because of it and pleaded, "Unless I get a break, I don't know what I'm gonna do." She was broke and cooking in her room at the elegant Astor Hotel on Broadway, right in the heart of the theatre district. The Astor was made famous by New Yorkers who met their dates under the clock in the lobby. Betty insisted she had to stay at the Astor, reasoning that, "You gotta put the dog on" (keep up appearances). Berman, observing her walking back and forth, all the while talking non-stop, suddenly put his hand up. "Wait a minute," he told her and telephoned his client, producer and songwriter B.G. DeSylva, in Florida where he was working on his latest musical comedy, *Panama Hattie*. DeSylva was to play a fateful role in the events that followed in the career of Betty Hutton – far more than anything he could ever have imagined.

Berman, completing his call to DeSylva, stopped Betty in her tracks when he told her he had the perfect part for her in *Panama Hattie*. One of the subplots of the musical was about blowing up the Panama Canal. Betty, in the part of Florrie, a dizzy canal zone soubrette, would play opposite Ethel Merman – the iron-lunged dame who introduced "I Got Rhythm," "Blow, Gabriel, Blow" and dozens of songs by Cole Porter and other songwriters.

On October 28, 1940, Ethel Merman's picture appeared on the cover of *Time* magazine. Not many Broadway personalities made that position in those days and Merman was called "the undisputed number one musical comedy songstress of these harassed times."

The year 1940 was the beginning of a decade of conflict. Just months before, dictator Adolf Hitler had led Nazi Germany on the road to World War II. The Great Depression was part of a worldwide collapse that brought dictatorship in many lands. Most Americans were preoccupied with making ends meet and they averted their eyes from fascism and aggression abroad. But they could not avoid the newsreels and radio that brought the world events into their homes. When, in September 1939, Germany attacked Poland, the two decades of peace between world wars ended.

B.G. DeSylva believed the popular song to be a barometer of the mental attitude of a country's people. If the songs are happy, the people are sad. If the songs have to do with financial embarrassment, then the people have money; when they sing of possessing money, they're broke. (Consider the hard acid rock of the '80s.)

Although this paradox of songs reflecting the opposing mood is not always true, nevertheless, Franklin D. Roosevelt, reelected to an unprecedented third term in 1940, did change the theme song of the country in 1933 from "Brother, Can You Spare a Dime?" to "Happy Days Are Here Again," whether true or not.

DeSylva also felt the same way about his protégé, Betty Hutton. An analogy of the times, Hutton – compulsive, hot headed, theatrical and full of fun – could be just the prescribed theatrical antidote, both sides of the Atlantic.

Americans, shattered by the news out of Europe, reacted to the RAF struggling with the Luftwaffe for mastery of the skies over England. The destiny of Britain had become a national obsession. Over 32,000 British children had been evacuated to the United States. The fall of France had inspired "The Last Time I Saw Paris," the battle of Britain, "A Nightingale Sang in Berkeley Square," and Tin Pan Alley was turning out "The White Cliffs of Dover" and Cole Porter composed "Make It Another Old Fashioned, Please," "Let's Be Buddies" and a host of other songs for *Panama Hattie*. Among the principals were Arthur Treacher, Rags Ragland and Betty Hutton, who had three numbers in the show: "Fresh As a Daisy," "They Ain't Doin' Right by Our Nell," and "All I Gotta Get Is My Man." Betty and the show's star, Ethel Merman, got along well enough except for one incident with conflicting versions.

Betty says, regretfully, "When I got in the show, Ethel took out my best number, 'Plant Your Own Tree.'"

According to Merman, "She [Hutton] had three numbers

when we opened in New Haven and the same three numbers when she withdrew from the cast to go into films. So why, years later, she tells everyone that I insisted upon her best number being cut, I'll never know."

One of the chorus girls in the show was June Allyson, who also became Betty's understudy when she proved she could do a good Hutton imitation.

When DeSylva took Betty to Hollywood a year later for a picture he was to produce, Allyson got her chance to go from understudy to featured performer. Eventually, she scored in Hollywood, as did a few others in the chorus: Vera-Ellen, Lucille Bremer and Betsy Blair.

Panama Hattie ran for 501 performances. During the run, her understudy took over for Hutton, who developed the measles. Just like in the movies, there was a famous director in the audience, George Abbott, who later signed Allyson for his next play, *Best Foot Forward*.

With some bitterness, Betty said, "When I left the show, June got her chance and I taught her everything she knew. She got this part in *Best Foot Forward* and I flew back [from the coast] to see her. I had a front row seat and I thought she would be thrilled. I brought her flowers. She didn't want to see me and she would never speak to me. I was hurt because I loved her. I thought she was so lovely. I don't know why she was ashamed to say I taught her. When she came to Hollywood, she didn't want to remember that. I can't understand to this day."

About this time, Hutton's mother suddenly stopped drinking, whether from a new feeling of security or to adapt herself to the new status. She could see now that her daughter was becoming an important star with all the problems inherent in that position. Sober, she could help her daughter. Betty bought her a new fur coat.

"When I was a little kid, my idea of success was to buy my mother a fur coat. I used to tell her, 'Someday, Mom, you won't have to work so hard and I'll buy you a fur coat down to the floor.'"

She bought her mother's first fur coat – though it was not "down to the floor," when she was singing with Vincent Lopez, earning $60 a week and supporting the family. "I paid $25 down and $5 a week. It was imitation black caracul." Mabel's new coat was a floor-length mink, just one of the many presents Betty gave her mother since her financial success, much of it thanks to B.G. DeSylva.

Paramount producer 45-year-old B.G. DeSylva gradually became the most influential person in Betty Hutton's life and career. He now cast her in her first important picture, *The Fleet's In.*

Buddy, as he was known, was born George Gard "Buddy" DeSylva in New York City. He began his career as a teenager in a dance band, as vocalist, and played the ukulele, like Mabel Hutton.

In 1939, he went from Hollywood to Broadway, where he packaged a trio of highly successful stage musicals, *DuBarry Was a Lady*, *Louisiana Purchase* and *Panama Hattie*. His first picture for Paramount, *Caught in the Draft*, with Bob Hope and Dorothy Lamour, was such a success he became the studio's Executive Producer in February 1941.

Events in Betty Hutton's life somehow always seemed to coincide with world-shaking catastrophes, as if an astrologer had deliberately arranged them. While she was making *The Fleet's In*, the Japanese bombed Pearl Harbor on December 7, 1941.

America's entry into the war brought escapist WWII comedy to an all-time high. Betty was certainly in the right place at the right time for the home-front musical comedy that came under the sharp influence of big time swing during the war years. The 1940 draft began removing the enormous number of males needed for dancers' ranks.

The forties jitterbugs stormed the Paramount Theatre in New York to hear Frank Sinatra and the big bands of Tommy Dorsey, Gene Krupa and Glenn Miller, with Marion Hutton as vocalist, and also to see the latest Paramount pictures.

Bing Crosby and Bob Hope dominated Paramount with their famous *Road* pictures with co-star Dorothy Lamour. The dressing room between them was appropriated by newcomer Betty Hutton.

Pranksters Hope and Crosby would meet their match in the merry madcap antics of the "Blonde Blitz" who combined the vitality of the Andrews Sisters and Abbott and Costello in one explosive package.

At the same time, MGM was about to launch 23-year-old June Allyson, who arrived in Hollywood for the movie version of *Best Foot Forward*. Lucille Ball would be its star. In her second picture at MGM, Allyson gave Mickey Rooney the "Betty Hutton treatment" in a specialty number, "Treat Me Rough," in *Girl Crazy*, which was an outright imitation; and she was rapidly on her way to enormous popularity, while the original 21-year-old Hutton became an instant hit in *The Fleet's In*. Betty's rendition of "Arthur Murray Taught Me Dancing in a Hurry," with Eddie Bracken in that picture, made her a star overnight, according to *Look* magazine.

"That was a big hit song. Johnny Mercer, who's the greatest songwriter of all time, wrote the score. But I don't think that alone did it. The role was funny."

Betty's role as Dorothy Lamour's boisterous man-hungry roommate was best summed up by *PM Magazine*; "Her facial grimaces, body twists and man-pummeling gymnastics take wonderfully to the screen."

From the time a star appears on the set, her steps are caged by chalk marks and focal distances, her voice is directed by microphones, controlled by dials and her image can only be seen if she moves with care within the cage. Obviously, Betty was such a wild creature, she couldn't be bounded.

Betty says Buddy DeSylva developed the three-camera technique because the director, Victor Schertzinger, couldn't make her hit her marks. "I don't know from walking in and looking down and all that jazz. They said to me, 'This is a long shot. Take it easy on the medium shots a little more. Close up, really go.' I don't know from that jazz. Every time I came out I was 'on.' I wanted to be great."

Schertzinger complained to DeSylva: "I can't hold her in the camera. She won't stay on the spot."

"I didn't hire her to stay on the spot," DeSylva replied. "I hired her because she is wild."

To solve the problem, DeSylva set up three cameras. "I only want one take from her because she gives it her all and she will not repeat it," he insisted. "I don't want it to be different. I want the instant reaction she feels."

There was also another problem. The hairdressing department decided to put "stuffing" in her curls to fatten them up.

"It's all gonna come out," Betty warned.

"We know better than you," they huffed back.

During the frenetic routine, the "stuffing" flew out all over the set and the director flew into a frenzy. Each time something went wrong, Hutton would seek out DeSylva and he would go to bat for her. His protective attitude fueled the growing rumors that they were having an affair.

Certainly, in DeSylva's eyes, Betty was unique: mercurial, waif-like, with a look of alarm hovering around her eyes; a hoyden, an undisciplined brat of incorrigible arrogance. She was blunt, un-ladylike, impatient with ambition. Yet she was anything but unfeminine; she had a sensuality all her own, an energetic sexy tomboyishness that appealed to many men.

"I was supposed to be 'that woman!' . . . Buddy was goin' with his secretary, who had a son by him, but his wife thought it was me. I was talked about all over the lot. Buddy's secretary lived in the same building as my mom and me. She needed a friend. Evenings all four of us got together."

DeSylva had been married to Marie Wallace since 1925, but they separated in 1944 and he fell in love with a former Ziegfeld showgirl who later became his secretary and bore him an illegitimate son.

"I had a great scene goin' with somebody else," Betty confessed. It was, no doubt, make-up director Perc Westmore. In 1942 he went overseas for Army duty and they announced their engagement. After he returned to the States to recuperate from a battle wound, the pending marriage was cancelled.

Betty was renowned for her overly romantic nature. With her great need for love, she often misinterpreted an affair for an enduring relationship. Fortunately, her schedule kept her so busy, she was able to avoid hasty mistakes.

Meanwhile, DeSylva guided her career at Paramount throughout her next films. *Star Spangled Rhythm* cast Betty as Polly, the irrepressible telephone operator at Paramount studios. *Star Spangled Rhythm* was made strictly as a wartime morale booster, using all the stars on the lot in various cameo appearances; brought together for the finale. A fantasy merry-go-round scene for the finale showcased stars Gary Cooper, Hope and Crosby, Dorothy Lamour, Alan Ladd and Veronica Lake, among others, and Betty Hutton. Figuratively, when the merry-go-round came to a sudden stop at war's end to re-shift its gears to reality, few of the popular idols were still aboard.

The film gave Betty a "hot" solo number, "I'm Doin' it for Defense." This time, director George Marshall had difficulty containing Betty's pyrotechnic talent within the prescribed camera range and he finally advised the lensman to follow her haphazard movements as best they could. *Happy Go Lucky*, starring Mary Martin, cast Betty as a jive singer, with her big number, "Murder, He Says," referring to the reaction of her boyfriend, Eddie Bracken. *Let's Face It* put her up against Bob Hope. As Winnie Porter, Betty, given the semi-glamour treatment, still got involved in a jujitsu bout with Hope, knocking his teeth caps off and scattering them over the soundstage.

"When they work with me," crowed Betty, "they gotta get insurance."

Hope quipped, "If they put a propeller on Hutton and sent her over Germany, the war would be over by Christmas."

The movie-going public found Hutton tremendous fun and

a perfect tonic for their problems at home. Besides getting loads of fan mail, she was named "A Star of Tomorrow" in 1942 by the *Motion Picture Herald's* Fame Poll. Her devil-may-care attitude and personality were the perfect reflection of the public attitude in the forties.

As part of her contribution to the war effort, Betty joined Fred Astaire, Lucille Ball, James Cagney, Judy Garland, Harpo Marx, William Powell, Mickey Rooney and, the most beloved by the public, Greer Garson, in a two-week bond selling tour in 1943.

While on tour, Betty telephoned Louella O. Parsons in Hollywood. Parsons, the "other" most powerful syndicated gossip columnist for the Hearst empire (the other being Hedda "The Hat" Hopper) had taken Betty under her "mother hen" wings.

Irrepressibly, Betty had told her one day: "Gee, when I read the headlines you have about my playing in Bing Crosby's next musical, I bought out the edition! I carried in the paper for my mother to see and I read your story so often I knew it by heart."

No words could ever warm Louella's heart more than having an actress confess she got a thrill out of being mentioned in her column. From then on, Hutton chose Louella over Hopper to fawn over. She got more press mileage from her and fell into an obedient line with: "Louella, I want you to be the first to know...," "which made the sob-sister practically wet her pants."

Betty, who was with the Hollywood Victory Caravan on a bond selling tour, telephoned from New York to tell Louella "she was the first to know" that she was going to marry Charles Martin in January 1943. Martin, formerly a Hollywood screenwriter, seen often in the company of Joan Crawford, was now writing radio scripts in New York and would follow Betty to Hollywood.

Soon afterwards, at age twenty-three, Betty, without real-izing it, was about to make a movie that would be the comedy hit of 1944 and one remembered especially by ex-servicemen.

Resident director Preston Sturges, whose satirical comedies have earned a place in film history, cast her as daffy Trudy Kock-enlocker in *The Miracle of Morgan's Creek*.

"We never had a script, never. Buddy had so much confi-dence in Sturges, it didn't matter. Sturges wouldn't tell us what the miracle was. He used to go to the studio each night to work on the next day's scenes. We had to be at the studio at 4:00 a.m., on location at 5:00 and then he'd sit around telling us how great he was 'til noon. Then we'd go to lunch. He owned the Player's Restaurant and, my God, they served these fantastic meals so we'd never get around to shooting 'till three or four in the afternoon. Then we would shoot 15 or 20 pages.

"I didn't know what the hell *The Miracle of Morgan's Creek* was. I didn't know I was goin' to have six babies."

As the plot unfolded, Trudy Kockenlocker gets drunk one night and wakes up the next morning thinking she had married someone called Private Ratzkywatsky. Later, when she discovers she is pregnant, she tells all to her 4-F boyfriend, Eddie Bracken, who agrees to marry. Trudy Kockenlocker subsequently gives birth to male sextuplets – the miracle!

Betty in a straight, non-singing, comedy role got praise indeed from critics and the public. There was even talk in the industry of an Oscar nomination. Sturges commented: "She's a full-fledged actress with every talent the noun implies. She plays in musicals because the public, which can do nothing well, is willing to concede its entertainers only one talent."

And the Angels Sing coasted into the Paramount Theatre on July 12, 1944. Betty stole the show with her rousing rendition of "My Rocking Horse Ran Away," which immediately became a trademark number. *The New York Post* explained: "Betty Hutton, it is perfectly clear, is the closest possible human approximation of a buzz bomb. Whether singing, dancing or making love to a helpless male, her preliminary whizzing assault is followed by an incomparable explosion." *The New York Times* wrote: ". . . if only the whole show were up to that number – 'My Rocking Horse Ran Away' – it would be a sensational affair."

If it were not for the "Buzz Bomb" Hutton and that particular song, Debbie Reynolds might not have had her own career in Hollywood.

Mary Frances Reynolds, a tiny 16-year-old, entered the Miss Burbank Contest in Southern California. The hyperactive bobby-socked tomboy tumbled out onstage and performed to a Betty Hutton recording, mouthing "My Rocking Horse Ran Away." The Girl Scout bowled over the judges, the audience and two talent scouts present. She won the contest and was crowned Miss Burbank of 1948.

"I won this contest," Debbie said, "and there were two talent scouts there, one from Warners and the other from MGM. They were old friends and flipped a coin to see which studio would get to interview me. Warners won. They put me under contract at $65 a week, although I'll never know why. About all I could do in the way of talent was to be exuberant – like Betty Hutton."

Some girls and boys, too, around the country were all doing their impersonations of Hutton at house-parties and high-school socials. For others, like June Allyson, and now Debbie Reynolds, it was the yellow-brick road to Hollywood.

Betty's contract at her studio now provided that she be paid $5,000 a week; this is 1940s' money, placing her in the top stable of Paramount stars. At this time, she was dating director Mervyn Le-Roy, now that her "trial engagement" to Charles Martin was over. She was close to her mother and sister but confided that for years, "I haven't had time to think about getting married. I had dates and I had fun. But I wanted a career first. Now, I have it. Now, I'm a star. Now I can look around. But the funny thing about it, when you get to this point, you suddenly realize that you are making so much money that there are only about ten men in the world that are making that much. Then, you gotta worry about *that*."

Her sister Marion made appearances in a few films at 20th Century-Fox but, under Betty's shadow, she found it difficult to develop a film career. Then, Buddy DeSylva thought of teaming Betty with her sister Marion in a musical, *My Sister and I*. Although he had to shelve the project when he became ill, he still kept watch over Betty's assignments. In *Here Comes the Waves*, Betty joined the Navy twice. She played identical twins in the picture – one blonde, the noisy one, and one brunette, the quiet one. Bing Crosby got squeezed between them both. She went on to make *The Stork Club* and *Incendiary Blonde*, and, like all of her pictures, this latter film proved to be another big moneymaker.

Betty was anxious to entertain the servicemen and they were anxious to meet "The Blonde Blitz," "Platinum Screwball," "Hectic Hutton," among other affectionate nicknames.

In July 1945, she embarked on a USO tour of the South Pacific and took her troupe to Honolulu, Johnson Island, Saipan,

Tinian, Guam, Antawarak, Namur, Tarawa, the Gilbert Islands, the Marianas, Roi and Majuro.

Betty proudly said, "I was in all the wars. I was in the South Pacific. I flew in with the guys. I didn't do what Bob Hope – whom I love – did. He would take a general's plane and cameras and bring his films back and sell them. I went on Army bucket seat planes and we flew in with the Japs actually firing at us. We had fighter planes. I coulda' been killed. Sometimes I'd do a show for maybe ten guys at a time 'cause you couldn't get a whole amphitheater together because the Japs in Iwo Jima were still there. So I was with the troops. I was in there, baby! I didn't go in *after* that island was secured.

"There were many unforgettable experiences in those days. I had a general's helmet on when I crawled into a dugout and when I took off my hat, the guys would say, 'Oh, my God!'

"It was such a kick for me. Then I went to Europe where I met Eisenhower. Eisenhower told me that if it weren't for *The Miracle of Morgan's Creek*, which his men had loved, he couldn't have won the Battle of the Bulge. That picture kept their spirits up and gave them much laughter before the last German offensive on the Western front." (December 16, 1944 through mid-January 1945.)

Betty stayed on to entertain troops in the Pacific area, traveling over 50,000 miles on tour. "At Saipan, they were still shooting. We moved around with 30 Marines as our bodyguards."

Exhausted and ill, refusing to give in for fear the tour might be cancelled, she kept her condition hidden as best she could. She wrote to her mother from an American base hospital in Saipan on October 28, 1944. "I got wonderful treatment and am okay but the doctor said if I hadn't improved in a couple of days, he would have me put on a plane for home. That would have broken my heart because some of the boys out here, particularly the Marines, hadn't seen a white woman for over two years. They almost cried when they greeted us."

Upon her return to Hollywood, she found her next project ready: *Duffy's Tavern* and, once completed, left for another USO tour to European Army camps, before recurring ill health cut short her activity and brought her back to the States. "I had a nervous breakdown in Paris because I had been working too hard. I had gotten an amoeba germ in the South Pacific, and you can't just ever find them. It's murder."

It was typical of Betty, who never became part of the swank Hollywood set, to fall for someone outside the profession. On September 2, 1945, Betty, then 24, was married at the Drake Hotel in Chicago to camera manufacturer Ted Briskin, age 28. (Coincidentally, they chose the same day that Japan signed the peace treaty and the fighting was over.) Theodore S. Briskin, president of the Revere Camera Company, married twenty years of show business with all the neuroses attendant to that profession.

"It was a pickup – plain and simple. Some friends made a blind date for me to go to the Pump Room for dinner. I peeked in and got a good look at my 'date' and said to myself, 'I can't stand that,' so I sneaked out, telephoned my hairdresser and met him at a restaurant called the Singapore, famous for its spareribs.

"We were not more than seated than I looked up and saw this guy. I had always laughed at that routine of somethin' 'electric' goin' through two people at the same moment, but it certainly did. He smiled at me and I smiled at him. I guess we flirted.

"I wasn't away long before my friends found out where I was and joined us and then we had a party goin'.

"I asked someone who was the guy I had been flirting with. I was told he was a Chicago businessman – and married. I said to myself, 'Anything that good lookin' has gotta be married or else a gangster.'"

The handsome stranger, who dined at the Singapore once or twice a week, asked the head waiter who she was. He said in astonishment, "Don't you know? That's Betty Hutton!"

"Oh! Introduce me, will you?"

"No, I can't do that," said the head waiter.

Discouraged, he decided to leave with his brother when the owner of the place stopped him. "Mr. Briskin, I have something to tell you. I'll call you about it."

"Tell me now," he asked.

"No, it will have to wait. I'll call you tomorrow."

As they walked out, he told his brother he was going back.

"Don't be a fool, she's just trying to use you for publicity," he told him.

Briskin went to a phone and called Betty inside the restaurant. She invited him to join her party. He did and later they went dancing.

"You know, I still thought he was a gangster and married and I insisted the next day that he show me his plant where he manufactured cameras. And, he wasn't married. I kept sayin' to myself: 'Nuthin' like that could happen to me. There must be somethin' wrong with this guy.' There wasn't a thing wrong with him as I could see. He was perfect."

"My family still had to be reckoned with," said Briskin, a Jew.

"To them, marrying an actress from Hollywood was something nobody in our family had ever done or believed possible, but my 96-year-old grandmother, who ruled the family, said, 'If you want to marry her, go ahead.' But I don't suppose anything in the world could have kept me from doing it. But Betty won the heart of my family and I didn't think religion was going to count, even though we were of different faiths."

Of course, Louella was the first to know. This time she really did wet her pants, as she was wont to do when very excited. This, and her drinking and her doctor husband, "Docky" as she called him, all became Hollywood legend.

Louella gushed to her millions of readers: "I was the first guest the newlyweds had in their California home, which I suppose was fitting since I was the first one to couple their names together.

"Betty had bought her house just before she met Ted and went overseas and it had all been done over in the gayest, brightest colors and the most modern of fabrics. Deep fuchsia and Kelly green dominate the living room; yellow is the color in the dining room and a profusion of reds, purples and yellows give a riot of color in the playroom. Only Betty's own bedroom is done in a delicate pale blue and pink.

"Ted is young, he's in comfortable circumstances, he's good looking and – best of all – he's crazy about Betty as she is about him – and that's saying a lot."

Betty didn't mention her plans for a family until Louella, seated on the newly-decorated sofa was safely in an upright position.

"The only thing we need now are three or four children."

Louella blushed and leaked the news in her column the next day: "That's news for Mr. Paramount who will probably faint with their best moneymaker star taking time out for motherhood with Dorothy Lamour and Veronica Lake already absent by an 'Act of God.'"

Hollywood, in particular, kept close tabs on Louella's column to find, heretofore, undisclosed gossip in the industry much more so than the current nationally televised *Entertainment Tonight*.

"ANNIE GET YOUR GUN"
An M-G-M Release

R62/102

```
                        BETTY HUTTON MOVIES


    1. The Fleet's In
       1942
       Paramount
       Running time: 93 minutes
       Songs: Build a Better Mousetrap
              Not Mine
              Arthur Murray Taught Me Dancing in a Hurry

    2. Star Spangled Rythm
       1942
       Paramount
       Running time: 99 minutes
       Songs: Doing It for Defense

    3. Happy Go Lucky
       1943
       Paramount
       Running time: 81 minutes
       Songs: Murder He Says
              The Fuddy Duddy Watchmaker

    4. Let's Face It
       1943
       Paramount
       Running time: 76 minutes
       Songs: Who Did? I Did! Yes I Did!
              Let's Not Talk About Love
              Plain Jane Doe

    5. The Miracle of Morgan's Creek
       1944
       Paramount
       Running time: 99 minutes

    6. Here Come the Waves
       1944
       Paramount
       Running time: 99 minutes
       Songs: The Fellow Waiting in Poughkeepsie
              Join the Navy
              I Promise You

    7. Incendiary Blonde
       1945
       Paramount
       Running time: 113 minutes
       Songs: Ragtime Cowboy Joe
              Oh By Jingo
              What Do You Want To Make Those Eyes at Me For?
              Row Row Row        It Had to Be You
```

```
                                          --2--


        8. And the Angels Sing
           1945
           Paramount
           Running time: ??
           Songs:   For the First Hundred Years
                    His Rocking Horse Ran Away
                    How Does Your Garden Grow?
                    Bluebirds in My Belfry

        9. Duffy's Tavern
           1945
           Paramount
           Running time: 97 minutes
           Songs: Doing It the Hard Way

       10.The Stork Club
          1945
          Paramount
          Running time: 98 minutes
          Songs: Doctor, Lawyer, Indian Chief
                 If I Had a Dozen Hearts
                 A Square in the Social Circle

       11.Cross My Heart
          1946
          Paramount
          Running time: 85 minutes
          Songs: That Little Dream Got Nowhere
                 Love Is the Darndest Thing
                 Chilly in Chile
                 How Do You Do It?

       12.The Perils of Pauline
          1947
          Paramount
          Running time: 98 minutes
          Songs: The Sewing Machine
                 Rumble Rumble Rumble
                 I Wish I Didn't Love You So
                 Papa Don't Preach to Me

       13.Dreamgirl**
          1947
          Paramount
          Running time: 85 minutes
          Songs: Drunk With Love
```

--3--

14. Red Hot and Blue
    1949
    Paramount
    Running time: 84 minutes
    Songs: Hamlet
           That's Loyalty
           Now That I Need You
           I Wake Up in the Morning Feeling Fine

15. Annie Get Your Gun
    1950
    MGM
    Running time: 107 minutes
    Songs: Doing What Comes Naturally
           You Can't Get a Man With a Gun
           There's No Business Like Show Business
           They Say That Falling In Love is Wonderful
           I'm an Indian Too
           Let's Go West Again
           The Girl That I Marry
           I Got the Sun in the Morning
           Anything You Can Do

16. Let's Dance
    1950
    Paramount
    Running time: 111 minutes
    Songs: Can't Stop Talking About Him
           Oh Them Dudes
           Why Fight the Feeling
           The Tunnel of Love

17. The Greatest Show on Earth
    1952
    Paramount
    Running time: 153 minutes
    Songs: Only a Rose
           Be a Jumping Jack
           The Greatest Show on Earth

18. Sailor Beware
    1952
    Paramount
    Running time: 108 minutes
    Cameo appearance

MOVIELAND'S
BLUE RIBBON
INTERVIEW

CONTINUED

"Cross my Heart" camera man gives advice to Betty and Sonny Tufts.

Above: Rodeo queen. Hutton is excellent rider, likes to do own picture stunting.

Platinum blonde locks are arranged while Betty talks to Director John Berry.

howling success. She also plotted, planned, and fought. In her own words:

"I've always said that talent alone wasn't enough. To get ahead in show business a person needs talent, sure, but he needs business ability and a

Thank heavens, you can do business even if you never majored in math!

great fighting capacity too. The one who hollers the loudest gets there fastest!"

Betty learned to "holler the loudest" during her pre-movie struggles—to holler literally and figuratively. Being a smart girl, she didn't drop her voice to a whisper when she hit Hollywood. Her raucous,

But once Hollywood hit me with laryngitis to my embarrassment—when I was on a personal appearance!

ear-tearing song style had been her fortune on the stage, and she brought it along to shatter more than microphones. Her frenetic, vitamin-charged delivery shattered records for quick stardom, too.

To those fans who have found her screen antics somewhat overwhelming and wearing, if intriguing, here is a happy thing to report: Betty Hutton is relaxing. On-screen and off. She is about through

Relaxing he says! and here I've just been sawed in half for "Perils of Pauline"!

Chapter Five

Throughout the forties and early fifties, Betty closely rivaled Judy Garland in critical endorsement and enormous fan adoration. In Berkeley, California, a devoted and sincere fan of Betty's has a room filled with her records, posters and mementos. George Moffett remains the best fan Betty Hutton ever had, then and now.

Like Judy, Betty required strong outside guidance for constructive channeling of her multiple talents. Other than from Buddy DeSylva, who now could not longer give her that needed attention due to his failing health, Betty would not accept the professional control she needed from business associates or her spouses. She wouldn't listen to her mother like she used to, or her sister Marion, who was having marital problems. On the surface, it appeared that Betty had at last had everything she ever wanted.

Having received *Look's* "Achievement Award" for 1944, she was voted "The Most Cooperative Actress of the Year" by the Hollywood Women's Press Club in 1945 and also was given a gizmo from the editors of the Marine Corps magazine, *The Leatherneck*.

She was in a powerful position at Paramount, at the box office where it counted the most; her pictures having grossed into
the millions of dollars.

After Buddy DeSylva retired as Paramount production chief, he
prepared several independent ventures for the studio. *The Stork
Club*, shot in 47 days, starred his favorite singing actress, Betty. The
critics seemed to agree that Betty, "the most vigorous worker in
the Paramount vineyard, practically blows her top in making *Stork
Club* an inviting entertainment." Her musical highlight was the
rambunctious "Doctor, Lawyer and Indian Chief."

The film opened at the Paramount Theatre in New York on December 19, 1945 and grossed $3.2 million in its national release. Betty
was rushed into her next quickie, *Cross My Heart*, spending as much
time off the set as she could with her mentor who was in ill health.

"Buddy had a long table in the studio commissary for ex-
ecutives. You could tell how your rushes were when you walked
in because he was either growling or smiling at you."

At lunchtime one day, Betty made her usual clarion-like entrance into the restaurant, greeting the Captain with her familiar,
"Hi ya, Dollface! Hey, ya got my table?" When she saw DeSylva
sitting with a group of men, she swung over to their table and
slid up forcefully right next to Cecil B. DeMille while greeting
everyone with the typical "Hello, Dollface."

"I didn't know who the hell he was, ya know. I knocked him
right on his fanny, picked him up and said, 'I'm sorry, sir!' DeMille silently composed himself and walked away, amidst an unfa-
miliar hush in the commissary."

"I thought, 'Oh, my God, Buddy doesn't like the rushes.' I
didn't know who DeMille was.

"Buddy said to me, 'Do you know who you just knocked down?'"

Every time she ran into DeMille after that incident, she grinned at him and yelled, "Hi ya, Dreamboat."

Cecil B. DeMille, born on August 12, 1881, practically built Paramount pictures with his enormous sex, sin and salvation film productions of the Bible, as rewritten by DeMille. The veteran producer-director was revered and treated like a biblical King himself. His closed studio sets and location shooting kept him practically apart from the other working personnel. His current spectacle, *Samson and Delilah*, in preparation, would be beyond the more commonplace bouncy Betty Hutton musicals.

Which leads us to the most talked about show on Broadway, a new musical by Irving Berlin, which opened at the Imperial Theatre on May 16, 1946: *Annie Get Your Gun*, starring Ethel Merman. After seeing it, Betty became obsessed with playing the part of the sharp-shooting Annie Oakley. However, that "Act of God" that Louella mentioned happened – Betty had her first child, Candy, on November 23, 1946.

Because of her pregnancy, she had to forego a guest spot in *Variety Girl*. But Paramount was preparing an extravagantly-mounted super-musical about the life of silent serial queen Pearl White for her return.

The Perils of Pauline introduced several songs, among them, Betty's "Pappa Don't Preach to Me," which became another big hit for her. The film was such a financial success that the studio developed more musical biographies for her. They announced projected film biographies of Clara Bow, Mabel Normand and Sophie Tucker. Sadly, they never came to be.

Cosmopolitan magazine chose her performance in *The Perils of Pauline* as best performance in musical comedy. At the same time, she signed with Capitol Records.

The critics were unanimous: "Betty Hutton grabs hold of the picture and squeezes all possible entertainment out of it." More B.G. DeSylva magic, *The Perils of Pauline* is seen repeatedly on television today as well as many of Hutton's movies. This particular movie is still a popular bestseller in the video market.

Betty gave birth to her second daughter, Lindsey, on April 14, 1948. Her pregnancy had cost her the starring role in Warner Brothers' *Romance on the High Seas* and had given Doris Day her first screen appearance as a Hutton replacement.

Warner Brothers producer Michael Curtiz hired songwriters Jule Styne and Sammy Cahn to do the score for the proposed Hutton vehicle; originally intended for Judy Garland. When Hutton's pregnancy cancelled her out, Cahn suggested Marion, an interesting idea which Betty would have applauded. However, agent Al Levy brought his client, a band singer, Doris Day to the studio for a screen test.

Jule Styne was at the piano, with Cahn standing by. Doris sang "(What Do You Do on) A Rainy Night in Rio," the same crooning way she sang before the microphone with the band. Those watching urged her to be more animated like, well, like Betty Hutton.

"Move around, you have to move," they coaxed. "Try to be more like Betty Hutton."

Obviously annoyed, not pleased with either the criticism or the comparison, Day replied rather petulantly: "Betty Hutton moves because she can't sing!"

On March 24, 1949, Doris Day sang, in her own way, "It's Magic," the Oscar-nominated song from *Romance on the High Seas*, at the Academy Awards ceremonies. Although the song lost to "Button and Bows," it made her and the picture she debuted in, an instant hit. Nevertheless, there is little argument that Hutton would have done it beautifully.

Doris Day became an overnight star with the public and press, falling in line with June Allyson and Debbie Reynolds, who took on a Hutton personality for their screen debuts. Day may have sung like Day in the film, but she acted like a subdued Hutton.

To show Hollywood she had arrived, Betty bought her first mink coat with a ten-dollar deposit, a Buick convertible and leased a penthouse. Now, with a tall, dark, handsome husband and two daughters, she moved into an eleven-room ranch-style house in Brentwood after weeks of preparation and decorating.

"They were all so happy," remembered her then-neighbor Kathryn Grayson.

Betty still maintained her non-stop fireworks display and brash-kid-sisterly appeal which the public adored. However, in thinking back, she said, "I never was sure of myself. I never understood how I became a star. I would look at Bing and Bob, all of them on the lot, and say, 'My God, I'm one of them!' I stared at them like lollipops – like a kid with his nose against the candy store window.

"But I wasn't happy. I had never been happy. I had always lived on Poverty Row. My goal was always to save my mother. I wanted my mother to be a lady. I wanted to meet the right people and read the right books. Even though I didn't have 'book learning,' as Annie would say. I learned from the greatest people in the world.

Bernard Baruch became a friend of mine. (Baruch was a financier and public official, who made a fortune on Wall Street and became an influential advisor to U.S. Presidents.)

"He was the great mentor to presidents. He was my teacher. I had to read the *New York Times* from cover to cover for him. Baruch was an advisor to F.D.R. I was invited to the White House because of him – three times. The Roosevelts were so kind to me and they gave me their governess for my kids.

"Education – sure, training – yes, still, you gotta have that gut feeling. Backstage you gotta have that. Only when the curtain's up am I happy."

A happy Betty went back to work after several months, to one of the most ambitious and expensive projects Paramount had ever had for her. The studio had paid $200,000 (in 1947 dollars) for the rights to Elmer Rice's arty stage success, *Dream Girl*, a fantasy drama. The public stayed away in droves, and the critics roasted the film in general and Betty in particular, with reviews like this: "Betty Hutton is a dud as the poor little millionaire's daughter who goes wandering in cuckooland." Badly miscast and directed, she said, "They took it apart because it didn't stick exactly to the play. That's a silly kick. Surely they must realize by now that you can't do the things of the screen [1948] that you can do on the stage. Every time that you hint in the movies that there might be such a thing as sex, the censors are on you like a tiger. Then you have to change the picture and when it comes out, the critics jump on you too, screaming 'This isn't like the play.'

"It's murder. You can't win against that combination. That's why I'm not doing any more film adaptations of the legits."

Then, Betty admitted to me, "I loused that movie up because I didn't understand the girl I was playing. But a Kitty Foyle, that kind of everyday girl, I could understand."

To hype box-office attendance, the studio sent its most potent asset, Betty Hutton, to San Francisco. *Dream Girl* was due to open at the Paramount Theatre there on July 4th holiday (1948) and combined with a personal appearance at the Golden Gate Theatre. Betty flew up to San Francisco. On arrival, she gave a luncheon for the press at her hotel, the Fairmont on Nob Hill.

The *San Francisco Chronicle* reporter Luther Nichols extolled: "Kansas has the cyclones, Italy has the Vesuvius, Alaska has the avalanches. And San Francisco, never to be outdone, now has its own display of spectacular natural energy in the shape of – and we do mean shape – Betty Hutton.

"Betty Hutton, who is like the Fourth of July 365 days a year, gave an informal and somewhat restrained exhibition of her fireworks in a press luncheon at the Fairmont.

"By this time most people must think of Miss Hutton (who insists, 'For gosh sakes, call me Betty') as a brash and brassy type, more clamorous than glamorous, something on the order of Texas Guinan, who she played in *Incendiary Blonde*. To hear her sing her most famous song, the eardrum eradicator 'Murder, He Says,' you could hardly think otherwise."

As the *Chronicle* recorded in 1948: "Even today, Betty could hardly be classed as an extrovert, but the 'new' Hutton subdued by marriage and motherhood (twice, both girls) is by no means a nerve jangler – just pleasantly uninhibited. And far from being glittery in looks, as you might expect after 16 years in show business, she has the healthy outdoor bloom of a 4-H club beauty contest winner."

"Guess what I weight?" Betty asked them, while spearing an-other leaf of lettuce from her salad plate. There were no secrets when Hutton was on with the press. They all underestimated.

"No, you flatterers. One hundred and thirty five. Isn't that awful? Every time I even look at a potato, I gain ten pounds. Honestly, I've been living on grass ever since Candy was born but nobody will believe me. Least of all my husband. I go all day with a watercress salad and a banana and he comes home and says, 'Say, why don't you cut down on the starches? You're get-ting fat.' How do you like that?"

Betty took this opportunity to inform the media, all dewy-eyed, that no matter what, "He's the nicest guy in the world."

Once you started Betty talking, it is like knocking the cap off a Market Street fire hydrant: the flow is steady, high-pressure and in all directions. Sophistication runs for cover but not com-mon sense. She is clever, disarming and totally winning with the press who feel they are old friends after sixty minutes.

Betty never failed to mention Buddy DeSylva. She was elated that DeSylva had, only recently, recovered from a long illness and happy about the prospect of working with him again. "He's the only producer who really understands me and knows what I can do." She repeated how he gave her a start on Broad-way, how he took her to Hollywood for her first screen role. She wouldn't know what she would do without him, what would happen to her career.

She concluded the interview by saying how she loved San Francisco audiences. "I was there once before, for a War Bond Rally at Civic Auditorium." She recalled her reception then and always looked forward to coming back.

Partly to get away from the sting of her only box-office failure to date, Betty went to London to appear at the Palladium, for $17,500 a week. This late 1948 stage appearance was a tremendous success. She loved the British audiences like no other, whose support and acceptance she found over the years were total and powerful.

Upon her return, Paramount, posthaste, tossed her into a more typical Betty Hutton movie, *Red, Hot and Blue*. For a change, Betty had a more virile leading man, Victor Mature, who would be Samson to Hedy Lamarr's Delilah that same year (1949).

Red, Hot and Blue was more like it; the way the public wanted Hutton. The critics agreed: "Betty Hutton, whose leaping, screaming, windmill style of song-and-dance delivery brings us images of a pogo stock in petticoats, is back again at her old stand."

In 1949, Buddy DeSylva had a plan to star her in a movie version of the silent vamp Theda Bara but Betty turned it down, in spite of her devotion to the producer. Increasingly beset with personal problems, a stubborn and expensive perfectionist, Betty found her confidence crumbled when Buddy DeSylva had a fatal heart attack.

"Buddy guided my career at Paramount," Betty told me many years later, with tears in her eyes. "Even then, after all those years, until he had a terrible stroke. When he died, the world stopped for me. That's when they first started bringing in independent producers. They divorced the theatres from the studios. Now comes the uncreative people that got money, they got gasoline stations (whatever), but what do they know about creative people? Nuthin'!"

Jane Fonda concurred with Betty's opinion. ". . . as with most of the major studios . . . they have been bought up by multi-national corporations and have become subsidiaries. For example, Warner Bros. is now a subsidiary of Kiddie Leisure and had questionable ownership itself linked with certain un-seeming areas. Paramount is a subsidiary of Gulf + Western, that multi-national corporation which controlled much of the economy of the Dominican Republic and owned vast numbers of oil shells off the coast of Vietnam during the war. In the time since I've been working in Hollywood, since 1958, the control of the movie industry has moved from the movie moguls, and as terrible as they were, at least they were movie makers. Now, it's into the corporate suites and the skyscrapers of the New York bankers. They're the ones who make the decisions."

Betty, who was there at that time, backed up Jane Fonda's comments: "That's what gave Buddy his heart attack, because of who they brought in. Hal Wallis was the first. Buddy had taken that studio out of the red and made it the number one gross-ing studio in Hollywood. When he died, I thought, 'What am I gonna do?' I kept turning down scripts right and left and, thank God, along comes *Annie.*

"Buddy had faith in me. What's more, he gave me faith in my-self. It was depression time for me when he died. If he had lived, I would have become a great dramatic actress because he was heading me toward that way; then the heart attack. He felt I really had that potential. He intended to make me into a dramatic star. I would like to do a great dramatic part in memory of him."

"ANNIE GET YOUR GUN"
An M-G-M Release

R62/102

THE PERILS OF PAULINE

VALLEY OF DOOM
EPISODE 4

VALIANT THEY CALLED HER—BUT BRAVE HEARTS, LIKE ALL RARE THINGS, ARE EASILY BROKEN . . .

● The mustachioed villain clutched Pauline's throat in a death grip, while hundreds of spectators looked on helplessly. At the height of suspense, a blurb flashed across the screen.

Will Pauline once more escape certain death?
See next episode of The Perils of Pauline
Friday at this theater.

After thirty years, it may be revealed that Pauline *did* escape. Again and again, through many a perilous serial. In fact, so indomitable was she in foiling the dastardly plots of her enemies that one hundred million Americans took Pearl White to their hearts.

Pearl's own heart was a brave one. But—as Julia Gibbs so often told her—brave hearts, like all rare things, are easily broken . . .

The stage had always been Pearl's dream. Ever since the day "Uncle Tom's Cabin" had played the small town where she lived. She hadn't seen the per-

Chapter Six

The star system that made Betty Hutton also made it easy for an actor to fall into a series of identical parts wherein the actor did not create the part but only exhibited himself, or herself. The studios manufactured dreams – motion pictures, with a celestial body of stars that fell to earth like fallen angels cast from a celluloid heaven as one after another, the studios collapsed and the gods they worshipped, the producers, died or were assassinated by corporations.

Ever since the opening of *Annie Get Your Gun* on Broadway on May 16, 1946, until it closed three and a half years later, Betty had been maniacal to win the lead in the projected movie version.

"I begged Paramount to buy it. I connived and pleaded and prayed for that part. They wouldn't because the price was too high." When MGM bought the screen rights to the smash hit play as a star vehicle for their Judy Garland, Betty was inconsolable.

"It's the biggest disappointment I've known. It's been my whole life and right now I know it isn't worth that. I thought a really big picture success would be the greatest thing in the world. But it's a rat race. No matter how good you are in one film, the next had got to be better. You've got to keep topping yourself or you're dead."

Up to this time, Betty had earned millions, but had not managed to save it, or her marriage. She and her husband, Ted Briskin, finally separated.

Betty, who when it was all summed up, made close to ten million dollars, tried to explain her financial losses: "I gave my money away to people that needed it. I had no love for money. Baruch gave up on me on that score. He was in the stock market. I don't know from money. All I know is if I'm great, they're gonna pay me. And I'm gonna spend it as fast as I can make [echoes of Judy Garland]. Talent is my social security. When I run outta talent, I'm dead." Ironically, Doris Day and Debbie Reynolds, as well as many others, lost a fortune not being able to account for their losses, except to say and write how their husbands had gotten them into debt through poor investments.

A very sick Judy Garland appeared on the set of *Annie*, more often than not, unable to work. Forcing her to go on in her pitiful condition only proved where the studio's interest lay.

"Judy finished the picture. [Actually, Garland only did a couple of scenes.] They saw it and knew it wasn't any good. They still tried to save it. I played golf with Eddie Mannix and L.B. Mayer, the studio chiefs. I bet them I'd be in it. They bet me $5,000. I said, 'I'll bet you never release that picture.' When they saw the final cut with Judy, they knew it wouldn't make it.

"Judy knew she was sick. I loved her 'til the day she died. And I was so fortunate to have gotten that part. They tested June Allyson, Debbie Reynolds – everybody. You name it. I made that bet – and I won. They would have to give it to me after all."

MGM went to Paramount to make the deal, to borrow her for the role. Paramount said, "No!" Betty soon found out about it. "I walked into the big shot's office and said, 'If I don't make this film, I'll never make another one here. I've been dyin' to do this film. It's mine!' You know how something fits you like a glove? Well, that was the way with this part."

They gave in, but never forgot. Neither did Ethel Merman. Hollywood had constantly ignored her when casting movies from her hit musicals. Except for *Anything Goes*, the roles she had created had always been awarded to other actresses: Kitty Kelly in *Girl Crazy*, Lillian Roth in *Take a Chance*, Lucille Ball in *DuBarry Was a Lady*, Ann Sothern in *Panama Hattie* and now Betty Hutton in *Annie Get Your Gun*.

Annie was beset by problems from the beginning. Judy had taken ill during the filming and her co-star, newcomer Howard Keel's, leg was broken when a horse fell on him. To add to this, MGM had to wait for Betty to finish her work on Paramount's *Let's Dance* with Fred Astaire, which wrapped up quickly so that the MGM production could proceed.

Fred Astaire later commented, "Working with Betty Hutton keeps anybody moving. She's so talented and conscientious that if you don't watch yourself, you feel you're standing still and letting her do the work."

Betty was in heaven. She loved the feeling of being sought after, being in demand.

"It was so much mine," she reiterated, almost as if the part of Annie could still be taken from her. "I didn't wear make-up in the beginning. Wally Westmore contrived a thing. We took wal-nuts and they put them in a blender, squeezed the juice outta 'em and they stained my skin with it and added more freckles to my own and that was my makeup. I played her right out of the backwoods, burned to a crisp. I didn't try to go for glamour – until I was a rodeo star; unlike the others who tested for the role looking like something from Rodeo Drive in Beverly Hills."

Howard Keel did not think much of Hutton, finding her "too self-centered" and "too concerned with her own performance rather than with the film as a whole."

In an interview with me he said, "She kept upstaging ev-erybody on the picture. Actually, everybody was upset with her. One day I found a spot where I could upstage her. She couldn't do anything about it. It was on a stairway. This is after weeks and weeks of – well – 'Go, let her do whatever she wants to.' I was a new face. If I have anything, it will come off. If I don't, I can have every foot of film and it won't happen. So we got to this place and it was 32 takes up and down the stairs. Finally, the director said, 'That's it!' Boom! I walked off and Lou Calhern, J. Carrol Naish, Ed Arnold and Keenan Wynn were all sitting there watch-ing. They said, 'If you had moved one inch, we would have killed you.'" Of course, Howard Keel went on to many other films at MGM and the national television series *Dallas*. *Annie Get Your Gun* did a great deal for his career.

Reminded that there were plans to re-team her with Keel (1967), 16 years after *Annie* in *Red Tomahawk*, Betty shot back, "NO! I would never have worked with him again. He felt he was a star at Metro. But you see, it's a woman's picture. No man could steal it. I don't care how good they think they are. It was Annie Oakley – *An-*

nie Get Your Gun, not *What's His Name – Get Your Gun*. He's been on talk shows and rapped me and rapped me because of *Annie*. He's still got that in his craw. I mean, that was a long time ago – 'cause he never made another great picture."

MGM's $3 ½ million *Annie Get Your Gun* debuted at Loew's State Theatre on May 17, 1950 and proved a blockbuster hit. The Technicolor song-filled show about a crack-shot tomboy Annie Oakley who joins Buffalo Bill's Wild West Show and falls madly in love with champion sharpshooter Howard Keel, was summed up in "There's No Business Like Show Business," the enduring hit from the show.

Dressed in buckskin, walnut-stained face, rifle at her side, Betty carried the musical over the top, dueting with Keel to "Anything You Can Do I Can Do Better" (perhaps with more truth than supposed), "You Can't Get a Man with a Gun," "I'm Am Indian, Too." Betty got unanimous raves from the critics for the first time. "That's the only one I got complete critical acclaim for," she said. "They said it was better than the play." I thought, "Oh boy, they're gonna belt me with this one 'cause Merman did it and Garland got it – the whole smear . . ."

The picture itself was called "Show business at its bright, gay, glittering best." Several critics remarked that Betty's style had not been popular with them in the past but now expressed admiration for her "great triumph," a rare blend of singing and acting talent.

Photoplay named her the most popular actress of the year and *Time* magazine featured her on its cover and wrote of her performance, "She lacks Ethel Merman's craftiness with comedy, but along with her unbridled vitality, she gives the role something brassy Ethel Merman never attempted – she kindles the love story into poignancy." (Considering her true feelings for her co-star, Keel, she should have gotten an Oscar.)

1950 began as the greatest year in Betty Hutton's life. There were lines forming at the box office to see her in *Annie*. MGM was so impressed by her sensational work they offered to buy her Paramount contract, but that studio adamantly refused. Betty was at her peak and they had no intention of letting her go. Her name was used in dialogue by William Holden in the classic film *Sunset Blvd*.

She was flooded with offers. The kid who sang in beer halls for nickels and dimes was besieged with million-dollar offers. Already a Capitol recording star, she signed with RCA Victor. Betty was on her way to increasing fame and fortune.

On May 21, 1950, five days after *Annie Get Your Gun* opened on Broadway, she starred for the prestigious *Theatre Guild on the Air* in a radio adaptation of an old Marion Davies movie, *Page Miss Glory*, with actor Ronald Reagan. While he was destined for historic immortality, she was headed for oblivion. But not before she had one more hit, The Greatest Show On Earth!

SCREEN ROMANCES

DELL

a

JULY
15¢

PERILS
OF
PAULINE

starring
Betty Hutton
John Lund

Chapter Seven

I'm ready for my close-up Mr. De Mille." Those words spoken by the deranged Norma Desmond, in the climatic scene from Sunset Boulevard, would become part of cinematic history and pass into the American idiom Betty Hutton would be repeating that line off camera, if she had her way, on her next picture. She was now the hottest and biggest star at Paramount. Despite the inroads of television, while other stars were being dropped from the studio roster Betty reached the top of the Paramount Mountain. After Annie Get Your Gun no one could believe she could go any higher. Betty wanted to top even herself and found a way to do just that.

Jauntily walking through a maze of clerical staff, while grinning a "Hello Kids!" Betty marched into the office of god himself, the revered and powerful Cecil B. De Mille, the man she had bumped onto the floor in the studio commissary. After a few "Hi ya dreamboat' greetings she and De Mille often dined together. Betty may have felt she would find in De Mille another rescuer to replace Buddy De Sylva. After many a successful cinematic schmaltz C.B. was also trying to outdo himself with a new epic in his colossal circus tribute.

Referring to the script of Greatest Show On Earth Betty got to the point. "Which one is the starring part? She blurted out," The elephant girl or the trapeze artist?"

"They are both equal, "C.B. intoned in that distinctive cultured voice.

Betty's eyes popped, "This I don't believe all ready".

Ignoring her, C.B. commanded, "Let me see your feet".

Surmising he had a foot fetish,   "I figured he was a feet-nut. So I took off my stockings. I have perfect feet- no bunions, nuthin. Of course I then realized he wanted feet that were beautiful, for the part of the trapeze artist-you know." What she didn't know was that C.B. had already decided on his Delilah, the stunningly beautiful Hedy Lamarr for that role. What C.B. didn't know was that once Betty heard about the picture she had already put a plan in action. All she had to find out now was which of the women's roles was the lead. "Well we hassled around a bit but De Mille still wouldn't come around and tell me."

As Betty walked out of the office the secretaries looked up and asked all at once," Did you get it?" Here was her chance. She stared at them quizzically. "The part?" "The part of Holly?" they implored. "Uh, huh," was all she could muster. Now she knew. It WAS the trapeze artist. She rushed to the florist. Together, following Betty's idea, they designed a gigantic orchid circus ring floral piece over sawdust flooring. Betty then placed a stuffed elephant with a blonde doll astride and another blonde doll swinging from a trapeze. The card enclosed read," Mr. De Mille my future rests in your hands. Which shall it be?

Like B.G. De Sylva, De Mille sensed greater talent in Hutton that her screen roles had provided. The fact that she would perform on a trapeze as well as sing was a key factor in her copping the prize plum when Hedy Lamarr rejected the part. Soon after wards he called a press conference to announce his cast for the Greatest Show On Earth: Cornel Wilde the aerialist, Charlton Heston the circus boss. Buttons the clown was James Stewart, Gloria Grahame as Angel, Dorothy Lamour as Phyllis and as Holly-Betty Hutton. Flattered that Betty had gone to so much trouble to get the part, she had been rehearsing on a still bar for weeks, notwithstanding her magnetic pull at the box office, C.B. knew she would work harder and take more risks than any glamour girl on the lot.

For much of 1951 Betty worked on the 151-minute production. Most trapeze performers start training when they are very young and Betty was a mature 30 at the time. She began her training with one of the greatest trapeze artists in the world Antoinette Conselhos of The Flying Conselhos. Just talking about it to me after all these years Betty became very animated. "When I was in the studio I was only 30 feet up in the air. It didn't frighten me so much. But I wanted to do it all. At the studio they had a belt around me. They have a caller who yells GO! and a catcher to grab you. There is only one instant where you must take off, or you miss him. Then you can only land from here to here (she demonstrated, shoulder to hip) or you break your neck or your legs. You don't get hurt in the air, it's how you land. If you miss that catcher....I hated that belt so I got that routine fast. GO! I took off. That guy who yelled out GO! from down below was called Toughie. He was from the circus and boy was he tough. Then we moved on location to Sarasota, Florida to the circus grounds, and into the tent. I looked up, and I looked up and I couldn't find the top. It's 60 feet up. I said to Antoinette I couldn't do it.

"My two little kids were watching me. All the circus tough-ies are standing around watching me too." Of sure, she's gonna do this-lots a luck. You could see it written on their faces. Antoinette knew I could do it. Even in front of the circus people, like I did at the studio." She said," If you don't get up there I'm going to kick you up all the way." We started up the ladder. It got hot, then hotter. I'm ready to faint so I sat on the bar. Now the catcher is all ready swinging reaching his orbit. I got up. I took the bar. They hollered GO! I took off – perfect- a marvel. I did my arabesque off the net with my hands, feet, perfect. You never heard such applause from the circus people. And they were tough."

Betty walked over to her two little girls, Lindsey and Candy," Well- how'd ya like Mommie?" They looked at her disapprov-ingly," Where's the music?" WOW! What a leveler. There's nuthin' you can do to please your kids." Both my arms had to be oper-ated on 'cause I hit that catcher at 50 miles an hour."

The picture swung into Radio City Music Hall on January 10, 1952. As Holly, the expert trapeze artist in love with circus boss Charlton Heston, Betty proved an engaging focal point. Whether vying with Cornel Wilde in daring high-bar stunts for number-one trapeze spot, or when the lion tamer causes the circus train to derail it is Betty's guiding spirit which pulls the circus troupe together to carry on the show and it is a massive bundle of crowd-pleasing "corny" entertainment. The Ringling

Brothers, Barnum and Bailey Circus elected her to its Hall of Fame.

As if to let me in on a long held secret Betty Practically whispered:" Sure the picture was a fantastic success. I co-directed it with De Mille. He asked me to. One day he said to me," Why haven't I ever gotten an award. My pictures make more money than any others."

Even then De Mille's films were colossal and stupendous, of the Biblical and ancient worlds, filled with golden bath tubs, marble pillars, thousands of extras, which packed them into movie houses, despite the homey TV sets It was hard to imagine someone like Cecil B. De Mille whose image as an arrogant type who threw his weight around, authoritatively giving orders through a megaphone, wearing jackboots, that became a cliché, asking for directorial support. He was 71 at the time and may have looked backed with some insecurity over his lack of artistic appreciation. As for Hutton I found her candor, her scorn of pretense, unquestionable. Perhaps because of her bluff exterior few who met her casually would notice her sensitivity. Her almost childlike simplicity, her direct honesty left no reason for disbelief.

Her answer to De Mille's perplexity was, "Mr. De Mille you're corny. Look - like in Unconquered. You got Gary Cooper and Paulette Goddard goin' over the falls in this little canoe to certain death. Out of nowhere, while they're falling Cooper catches hold of this little twig with one hand and Goddard with the other. The canoe goes to its destruction and they are saved by this twig and climb up a mountain side to safety. That's ridiculous!"

"I win my awards at the box-office," declared De Mille.

"Yeah, sure. Your pictures make a fortune, which goes to prove that people love corn. The circus is corny-leave it alone. Just do the story like it's written. Don't add to it."

According to Betty she sat beside DeMille every day, looked through the viewfinder, made suggestions, discussed scenes and generally co-directed. Often Betty would kid C.B. to relieve the tension she felt building up calling him her lover on the set. On day on the set while seated next to him she saw him grimace and suddenly start to fall over. She caught him just in time. A few standing by rushed over, Betty ordered a brandy, quick, but keep it quiet. The girl said but he doesn't drink. "Get him a brandy fast and keep it quiet. She then joked with him, "Hey, lover a little tired from last night. Too much for you, huh?" De Mille responded to the cue-pulled himself together, drank the brandy and confided to her," Betty I've had a little heart attack. I'm all right. Just a bit of a strain. Don't say anything about this. Let's keep it between ourselves. Soon after, De Mille picked up his megaphone and directed right into the night. (Several years later De Mille died of a heart attack on January 21, 1955) CB had to wait 20 years after he produced the first 4 reel feature in film history- to win an Academy Award, on March 19, 1953. Betty cried 'like a baby' watching him get his Oscar at long last. "He sent me a 10 page letter," she said, right after saying I should have gotten half of that award. They run Greatest Show and Annie all the time. I have fans that are kids. They must think I'm still 19 years old. Which is groovy."

Ruth Gordon, Oscar winner for *Rosemary's Baby* (1968), and her husband Garson Kanin, playwright and director, were in San Francisco, in 1976 staying at the Huntington Hotel on California

Street across from Huntington Park where they could watch the cable cars roll by on Nob Hill. Ruth was promoting her book, *My Side*. We had spoken on the telephone previously to schedule an interview for my national radio show for PBS, with the husband-wife collaborating team. Our time schedules crossed over and we didn't make it. However, Ruth Gordon left her book, *My Side*, for me at the front desk of her hotel and a double-signed autograph picture of herself and her husband. In one of our conversations, *Born Yesterday* was mentioned.

Columbia Pictures mogul Harry Cohn had paid a million dollars for the movie rights of Kanin's play as a starring vehicle for his biggest asset, Rita Hayworth. But Rita was in love with Aly Khan which precluded everything else. Meanwhile, Judy Holliday was a big hit on Broadway in the part, a comedienne who played Brooklyn-accented, dumb broads (successfully in *Adam's Rib*). Betty Hutton, at the time about Judy Holliday's age, was riding high after *Annie Get Your Gun* and *The Greatest Show on Earth*, and Ruth Gordon wanted her to play Billie Dawn, the shrewd dumb-blond in the movie version of the play. Had Betty Hutton known this, she would have gone all out to get it. Kanin, who usually listened to his wife's advice, for reasons unknown, perhaps abetted by director George Cukor, a friend of Holliday and Cohn, let it pass.

On Academy Award night, in Hollywood, March 29, 1951, unbelievably, Judy Holliday won the Oscar over Gloria Swanson (*Sunset Blvd.*) and Bette Davis (*All About Eve*). And Betty Hutton, most likely unbeknownst to her, may have missed out on her one and only chance to be enshrined as an Oscar winner advancing her career to new heights rather than the downslide she would soon face.

From here on her demons pursued her. "The scripts were gettin' worse and worse. When I'm working with jerks with no talent, I raise hell until I get what I want." The studio listened. In the classic *Sunset Blvd.* (1950), a down-at-the-heels screenwriter (William Holden) tries to sell a baseball story to a Paramount producer as a vehicle for Alan Ladd. "Of course, we're always looking for a Betty Hutton," he said. "Do you see it as a Betty Hutton?" This dialogue summed up the studio's problems with its Blonde Bombshell. Vehicles were becoming increasingly difficult to find and that she would accept. But Betty's war with Paramount was ongoing. In 1951, when "In the Cool, Cool, Cool of the Evening," a song written especially for her, was given to Bing Crosby for the film *Here Comes the Groom* (and won an Academy Award) Betty's rage was deafening. She finally refused to accept any of them. "They were rotten," Betty fumed; "One was *The Keystone Girl*." (In the author's opinion, her refusal of the role was a big mistake in judgment on Betty's part. The film was a biography of Mabel Normand, the silent screen's popular comedienne, who quickly became Mack Sennett's biggest star. Composer Jerry Herman's musical, *Mack & Mabel*, about the star-crossed lovers, today is a cult classic.) "I was under a terrific contract at Paramount. I got $5,000 a week, 52 weeks a year. They couldn't take me off salary if I turned the script down. I felt embarrassed. I just couldn't just go on takin' that money."

"I followed Judy into the Palace [1952]; I broke her record [Betty's 4-week stay was a sell-out], which they didn't think could be done. But I didn't get critical acclaim for it; I'm not a critic's performer. Critics don't dig me. The people dig me, and that's more important. The critics sit there on their duffs and say, 'Well, I don't know that she's chic enough for me to give a good review to.' But the audience is goin' wild!"

As a result of the arduous Palace Theater stint, Betty lost her voice, and it was disclosed that she had a growth on her vocal cords. After the operation, she went into rehearsals for her new Paramount musical, *Somebody Loves Me*. It was loosely based on the vaudeville careers of Blossom Seeley and Benny Fields. The Technicolor movie starts in 1906 on San Francisco's Barbary Coast. It was while working on that movie that she met Charles O'Curran.

Charles O'Curran came to Hollywood in 1944. He was born in Atlantic City, New Jersey. He started in the entertainment field as a saxophonist and clarinetist before he organized his own band. At 19 he went to Paris and danced with the Follies Bergere. From there he went into Vaudeville, eventually turning to the production end of the business.

After her divorce from Ted Briskin Betty sighed that she sure missed the state of matrimony; but, undeterred, she had a number of on-and-off again romances. "I don't enjoy being single," she repeatedly said. Choreographer O'Curran overheard and moved fast. One night over dinner, on March 18, 1952, they decided to elope to Las Vegas. They flew there from Hollywood at 10 p.m., arrived at 12:30 a.m., by 1:00 a.m. they were married. The couple said their honeymoon would have to be delayed. They had to return to Hollywood so that Betty could polish up her dance routines for her Palace Theater engagement in New York in two weeks. Now, Betty was determined that her new husband would stage all her acts. And direct her next picture. After all, as he said, he was an actor, choreographer, dance director and motion picture director among other things. Fine, thought Paramount, he can find work elsewhere, easily

They offered her another great story, the life of The Duncan Sisters – *Topsy & Eva*, co-starring Ginger Rogers. And, again, Paramount refused her husband as the director. But Las Vegas came calling and was offering Betty Hutton $100,000 a week. So, Mrs. O'Curran took it and said to Paramount, "I don't want any more of this scene. SHOVE IT!" At this time she had earned the reputation of being bitchy, willful, petulant and lithesome. The priceless jewel of stardom, for which she gave her soul, seemingly turned into a tinsel ornament. Betty walked out and drove through the Paramount gates, which slammed behind her right into a blacklist. Her friend, composer Sammy Cahn, confided to me on a radio broadcast, "Never have I seen someone like that rise to the top so fast and self-destruct; she went up like a rocket and came down to disintegrate."

When Betty walked out, July 10, 1952, Paramount subsequently hired the popular songstress (with a little help from Bing Crosby) Rosemary Clooney to perform in its declining number of musicals.

Direct from the London Palladium and the New York Palace to the Curran Theatre, on January 19, 1953, Betty and her International Variety Revue opened at the Curran Theatre, in San Francisco. Bride and bridegroom, now producer and director of choreography, went into business for themselves (who needed Paramount) for the first time with a variety show. Their Lindsey Corporation was named for Betty's oldest daughter. Charlie O'Curran ran the whole show, including designing the sets and scenery. Edith Head, from Betty's old Paramount days, got to design her costumes. Betty's mom, Mabel, who always traveled with her, hung around the dressing room, offering her help and chatting away with visiting reporters. Mabel said "Betty always had a way of expressing herself. As a baby, she'd get on the kitchen table and sing and dance while I played the guitar. Her father, Percy, and I, sang too, and I played the piano by ear." Betty piped in, "And my father and mother always played for square dances in the Little German community where we lived in Nebraska. We're the American success story. It doesn't matter if you come from the wrong side of the tracks, if you work hard and deliver . . . " Mabel Hutton added, "I have a new fur coat and a new home Betty just bought for me in North Hollywood. But I haven't had time to furnish it yet. It's gonna be provincial - sort of Early American."

Mabel Hutton was the show's chief dresser with responsibilities for the costumes of seven people. "Betty's room is a bedlam, when she gets out of it," said Mabel. "And her dressing room at the theatre—that's murder! Some day, she added, 'If I can retire, I'll be a housefrau. I have a husband you know, Gilbert Adams. I was remarried in 1942. But in the meantime I had to get down to the theatre early. Betty's hat for the New Orleans number needs a new red feather and I have to fix the pink dress. The trick purse has to be checked to be sure it works. And I had to take care of the Five Skylarks, too, we don't want any zipper trouble." And off she went.

Whatever she did and wherever she went, Betty broke box-office records.

Back to London's Palladium, she was an even bigger hit than before. Now she was ready to conquer a new upstart. On September 1, 1954, she made her television debut in one of the biggest bombs in the history of entertainment, *Satins and Spurs*, the first

in a series of 90-minute musical "Spectaculars" created by producer Max Liebman. A series of other failures followed, affecting
her already volatile nervous system, and setting off a frenzied reaction increasing her already serious intake of pills and alcohol. She
placed a lot of blame on her second husband.

Betty began the New Year of 1955 by divorcing O'Curran.
Within weeks she leaped into another "nuptial tie" with a
Capitol Records executive, Alan W. Livingston. She could not
be alone. Her husband's dependency became neurotic. She
couldn't stop working either. She reappeared on television as
star of an hour special, with guests Bob Hope and Jimmy Du-
rante. She worked hard - too hard – and it showed. Meanwhile,
Judy Garland, slated for another film comeback at United Artists, faltered. And, like some psychic shadow, Betty stepped in
again as her replacement. Strangely, *Spring Reunion* opened at
the site of her past triumph, the Palace. It failed. At best, new
movie offers would be very far and few between. As Betty considered herself a religious person outwardly, who didn't belong
to a church, Dr. Norman Vincent Peal's "The Power of Positive
Thinking" led her to join the Lutheran Church. She knew she
needed help from somewhere, and she would make a deal with
anyone to get it. Spiritually, she wasn't ready. As doors closed,
she looked for others to open.

CBS-TV offered Betty a show of her own. To celebrate, she
had a bar installed on the set and at 4 p.m. every afternoon it
was party time. Enthusiastic about the show she said, "It's so
cotton-pickin' full of fun; you'll die when you see it." That's ex-
actly what happened. It died and was buried in the spring of
1960. Disgusted, Betty threw Dr. Peal's book out the window.

"I couldn't stand by while a bunch of rank amateurs from the advertising agency tried to ruin the show." Her hard-to-take failures spilled over into the fast lane of parties. "I was on a lot of speed," and she was moving fast, all right, but where to? She, least of all, didn't know.

Twenty-three months later Betty quit show-business. At 33 she sang her swan song at the close of a 4-week engagement at the Las Vegas Inn. Betty openly confessed, to the audience, "I'm through, finished, washed up, ended. How final can you get?" Everybody, from the audience to the waitresses, parking lot attendants and powder room staff, cried. It was a very tearful farewell. Her variety show failed, her TV spectacular *Satins and Spurs* flopped, as did her marriage to O'Curran, who masterminded her career. So what does a retired performer, like Betty, do? Well, she got herself a new agent.

Chapter Eight

Three months later a very bored Betty was back to work. "I tried staying home to care for the kids but that was a flop, too . . . bein' a den mother to the Brentwood Brownies just ain't my style, with the energy I got, sittin' around was rough." Always newsworthy, in September 1960, Betty gave the fourth-estate something else to scandalize about. A wild feud erupted between Betty and TV host Jack Parr over his national late-night talk show. And just weeks later, on October 21, 1960, Betty divorced Livingston. Each charged the other with mental cruelty. Now, a carefree Betty gifted herself with another new man for Christmas. On December 24, 1960, Betty, 39, and trumpeter Peter Candoli, age 37, were married in Las Vegas at the Lutheran Reformation Church. She had known the musician for the past 12 years. He had a daughter, Tara, by a previous marriage. The press continued to follow close behind her troubled heels. They didn't have long to wait.

January 1962 began a further decline. Her mother Mabel burned to death in her Hollywood home. Her lit cigarette, when she fell asleep, set the house ablaze. Mabel had been her constant companion because, she once explained, "Anyone else would drive her crazy." Actors Equity fined her for being uncooperative during a summer stock tour of *Gypsy*. She dropped out of a new vehicle, *Calamity Jane*, when she became pregnant (Ginger Rogers substituted for her in the role). Finally, the sun broke through as Betty gave birth to her third daughter, Carolyn, in 1962. She even got back on Broadway when she took over the Carol Burnett part in the stage musical, *Fade Out-Fade In*, for one week, while Burnet took a much needed rest. However, poor attendance proved how her box-office appeal had shrunk.

For the moment, a *Gunsmoke* TV episode came along on May 1, 1965. Although it was an extremely popular series, her supporting character role in it showed how her once superstar status had faded. With money running out she was ready to take any offers. She signed for two quickie low-budget westerns in 1967. One, *Red Tomahawk*, would have reunited her with Howard Keel, her detested Frank Butler from *Annie Get Your Gun*. She found him even more repulsive than before, and quit the picture.

Then, on June 9, 1967, Betty declared bankruptcy, listing debts in the thousands, as well as stating that she was behind in her rent. All this from a woman who had earned over ten million dollars in her lifetime. Now, all was lost. "It's been a nightmare," she said. "I lost my mother, my two older girls walked away from me. I had a bad marriage, my career stopped, except for summer stock at some cockamamie places I would never had been booked in before. And once you accept one of those, zoom! Down the tube . . . I mean it's amateur night in Dixie." She had lost it all. In a futile search to win back part of it, she became a spirit of frenzied activity. She could not get off nor give up the violently galloping "Rocking Horse" fame of her former stardom. Instead, she clung to it in desperation.

To add to everything else, her private life was a mess. She had continual, sometimes violent arguments with her husband, Pete. At one time he attempted to kill her. After every crazy separation, there followed a passionate making-up. She was terrified of losing him. She loved him more than the others, she said, believing he was all she had left to live for. Then, alone in bed one morning, after a particularly great night of Candoli lovemaking, she heard on the radio, gossip columnist Rona Barrett revealing that "Betty Hutton's husband, Pete Candoli, was secretively engaged to blonde entertainer Edie Adams." Further break-ups and reconciliations ensued, until, exhausted, they finally obtained a Mexican divorce in November 1971.

Chapter Nine

Betty was melodramatic in her anguish; she raved, she ranted, she cried for hours. To her it was the end of everything----love, career, ambition, the world. There was only one thing for her to do . . . to go on being Betty Hutton the way she thought the public wanted her. "I still get fan mail," she said pathetically. She did everything she could to live up to her bombastic image and dying in the attempt. Her drive for "fun" and diversion from everyday reality is as old as sin. Estranged from family, friends, Hollywood, and life - the Incendiary Blonde was burned out! At the age of 45, Betty' Hutton's life was over - or so she believed. She had tried to kill herself before, but this time - this time - she was determined to succeed. Actually, it was to be a new beginning. Now, she was spiritually ready.

"I tried to kill myself all over New England," she told me. "I wanted to escape after my last marriage broke up, which was a nightmare. I ran! But it was not God's intention. They took me to a 'detox' in Massachusetts. And one day, Father Peter McGuire, who headed the center from Newport, came for a visit. And I met Father McGuire," her voice rising. He didn't know Betty Hutton from a bale of hay. He'd never seen a movie of hers. "He is as Christ-like as you can be. He taught me this love, to not be so hurt inside. I'm writing a book, *Backstage, You Can Have*, about when the curtain comes down and you're left alone. And that great love that you just had [from the audience] is gone. They raise the curtain, all the people are gone. I walked around and felt the seats, they were still warm, and I looked up at the stage. The guys were mopping up the dreams that just happened, between you and the audience. Anyway, I looked across the room, in rehab, and said, 'That's the man who will save my life . . .'"

Father McGuire asked Betty to come to Portsmouth; she would have a little cottage to live in behind the rectory of St. Anthony's Church. And she would have a job. "I cooked, did dishes, made beds, I wanted that refuge of being with spiritual people. We used to have a ball in that kitchen. I used to sing all the dirty parodies my mother taught me. I'd be doin' dishes, and that really is boring, you know. I didn't realize Fr. McGuire had brought some people in, and I was singing out loud, while scrubbin' pots."

Two old maids in a folding bed,

One turned over and the other said,

Yes . . . we got no bananas, we got no bananas tonight!

I started to do a little dance, and I turned around and saw Fr. McGuire, Father Hamilton, and these very proper ladies standing there. I gulped, 'Oh, my God,' I died." I was so happy there before the news got out to the papers. Then the world came." The rectory soon became filled with fan mail, but all of that media frenzy further embarrassed her family. Her scandalized behavior drove her children even further away from her. "I lost my kids . . . I wasn't in my right mind. My children growing up were very angry with me all the time. Because they didn't know what was happening to me, emotionally. They just thought I was crazy and were afraid of me. I wanted them to leave because I couldn't take care of them. I was married to Candoli at the time. I let Lindsey go to her father, Ted Briskin. Candy, whose father was also Briskin, went to live on a ranch with a family she knew. I thought of my daughters every day and my daily prayer was, *God, just let me see them once more*. I had just turned 59 and I wanted to talk to my daughters before it was too late."

Finally, with the Church's help, Father McGuire one Christmas arranged a reunion with their mother. "When Lindsey called, we both sobbed, then talked for hours. It was the first time in 10 years we'd spoken to each other." However, her sister Marion said later that Betty's downfall came about because she blamed everyone but herself for her problems. An example of what stardom can do to the unrealistic and immature.

All the world-wide attention from the press and the public made the attempt to rebuild her life difficult. "Some days I cried, this won't work." Her psychiatrist committed her to Butler Hospital in Providence (December 1974) for a complete checkup. Once Betty was back at the rectory, Fr. McGuire received that telephone call from San Francisco with yet another chance for a theatrical comeback . . . and this is how and where this author and Betty Hutton met.

When the proposed plan to bring Betty back to the Golden Gate Theatre in *Fallen Angels* had reached a dead end, Betty refused to return to Portsmouth. She had wisely held onto her return airline ticket, in a way, refusing failure that was not hers. It was strictly financial. Producer Cliff Reid couldn't raise enough money. The Golden Gate was too big a house, too many seats; it was an intimate comedy and had he tried for a smaller theatre it may have worked.

To cheer Betty up, during an interview I had with Ginger Rogers for PBS (who was then appearing in the Venetian Room at the Fairmont Hotel), I talked to Ginger about their getting together. She arranged ringside seats for the next night's show. Betty, in a newly designed white chiffon dress made especially for her by a friend of mine, looked wonderful. During the show Ginger introduced Betty to the audience from the stage, and Betty jubilantly responded by joining her in the spotlight. They exchanged some old-time memories about their days at the studios. And regretted they did not make *Topsy & Eva*, the life of the Duncan Sisters, and so forth. Ginger gently tried to wrestle the microphone from Betty, but she was too excited to let go. I started to applaud and it broke the tension. After the show we joined Ginger in her suite, among other guests, and Betty left excited and happy. Betty called me the following morning all fired up. "I just talked to Ginger and they want us for *Arsenic And Old Lace* . . . we are going to be dynamite in that movie!" Betty continued, elated," Ginger and I look alike; we think alike, we love God. It doesn't matter what religion [Ginger was a Christian Scientist] as long as your heart is that way." I didn't speak to Miss Rogers about it, and no more was ever said on that subject by Betty.

Then, seemingly, an old romance, with a young man, suddenly appeared from out of San Carlos, down the peninsula . . .

and he and Betty became engaged. She wanted me to meet her next husband, whom she claimed to have known years before. (He was so young that he must have been 12 at that time). Driving down the peninsula, I witnessed their loving reunion (photographed for posterity), except there was a fly in the ointment. Her fiancé's roommate, who was also a producer of sorts, had wanted to finance a new nightclub act for her. However, his resentment over losing his lover to Betty cancelled all plans forthwith, including the proposed nuptials. On the drive back up to San Francisco, Betty unbelievably asked me to marry her, I suppose as a consolation prize. I told her she had enough problems; she insisted, and I felt dark clouds approaching. Another broken romance . . . and knowing that Ginger Rogers who, although much older than she, was still working, set her to reliving her own lost lovers and career.

Becoming increasingly disoriented, Betty started slipping back. The ensuing weeks brought on a tragic-comedy chain of events. Moving from one place to another as a "house guest" (more of a party prize) she finally wound up in the hands and home of an unscrupulous male fan, Richard Moore. He immediately cut off all communication between us, although Betty (rejected or jilted as she said), wasn't willing to see me at that moment. Her host eventually sold her story of her present setback to the *National Enquirer* (12/20/1977) for $5,000 without her knowledge. He had secretly taken snapshots of her. When the story broke headlining Betty with a full-page cover spread, she looked for an escape. Shattered by the whole experience of her misadventures in San Francisco, she left town for the sanctuary of St. Anthony's Parish and Father McGuire . . . and never even said good-bye, to me.

Chapter Ten

St. Anthony's Church (the patron saint of lost souls), welcomed back one of their lost sheep. Betty Hutton, again, was pouring coffee for the Rev. Peter J. McGuire and Rev. James J. Hamilton in the rectory kitchen as she had done so many times before. She felt she was home, among simple, uncomplicated people. She leaned on Fr. McGuire for spiritual strength. He was her Guardian Angel and counselor. She would talk to him for "hours at a stretch," she said, often repeating the same mantra. "I told him of my goal to save my mother; I wanted her to be a lady." Then came the breaking point. She was haunted by her mother having burnt to death in a fire 24 years ago. "Investigators told me she had dropped a lighted cigarette on a couch and fell asleep. That was the beginning of the end for me." The rest was all too familiar to him by now.

To me, she acknowledged that money doesn't bring you joy. "Hey, I knew Doris Duke, one of the richest women in the world." With this statement she brought to mind a story I had heard, from a reliable source. When Doris fired her longtime secretary, Kate Bourne, the first person to replace her was Betty Hutton, who was then derelict during the '70s and '80s. Betty had been to the Duke Farm estate many times, and had known Doris for decades. Doris decided to help Betty out and, besides, she needed new help and an old friend. The job lasted less than a week as Betty was too strong willed despite her circumstances. Betty outlived her old friend as Doris Duke died at 80 years old in 1993.

Betty had been to the Duke estate many times as a little girl, she told me, that during the brief sojourn at Duke Farm Betty wanted to see the indoor pool and tennis courts she remembered. When she was ushered into the area the sight of the dust-covered golden relics before her eyes caused her to laugh hysterically. The half-finished clutter of treasure struck her as the most anachronistic, incongruous display of utter selfishness she could ever imagine.

"Sure, there were times that I was bitter," she said, about her life at the rectory. "I lived in a dark attic on the rectory's third floor [or a cottage behind the rectory]. I felt like Cinderella must have felt sweeping up ashes." And, magically, like Cinderella, she was invited to a ball. The ball was to be held, not at a castle, but big enough, the Empire State Building in Manhattan at the Riverboat nightclub. Celebrity friends organized a "Love-IN"; proceeds from the $100-a-plate dinner would go to the St. Anthony's parish. Around 400 guests were invited; about 30 parishioners missed the pumpkin and went by bus to pay tribute to the parish housekeeper.

Wearing the white chiffon gown she wore to the Ginger Rogers show, with a new bouffant hairdo, long eyelashes, the guest of honor glowed, alternately laughing and crying as tributes came from George Jessel, Sammy Cahn, Arlene Dahl and many others. Before the stand-up microphone, in a soft pink spotlight, Betty was "a star" again, until midnight. "I love you, I love you all," she told her friends, throwing kisses. But, she made it clear that this was only a one-night stand in New York and that she was going back to Portsmouth. Back to washing dishes as housekeeper-cook at St. Anthony's." Of course she meant it at the time, but something happened that night that would change her mind, and thus altered her course.

"Betty Hutton is through at the rectory," Fr. McGuire told inquirers. "It didn't work out. She's only 53. She is still young. She's not ready to retire. She'd like to get back into show business, and get started again."

An old arm injury, suffered while working the bar in the circus extravaganza, *The Greatest Show on Earth* started acting up again. She entered Butler's Hospital Treatment Center in Providence and was released from the hospital on New Year's Day, 1975.

Benny Venuta, a friend of Betty's in their Broadway and Hollywood days, was one of the crowd cheering for Betty at The Riverboat "Love-IN" party. They had been in the movie version of *Annie Get Your Gun* together. Benny told the press, "I went to see her in the hospital a week ago Sunday. She looked marvelous. [Betty didn't mention a face lift.] She didn't say anything about going back in show business, but I know she'd love to get a job." What she didn't say was that night rekindled the old theatrical flame and she had never been the same since she left New York and returned to Rhode Island. The next few years she was preparing for another comeback. Wanting to give it a try, one more time as a singer. And bang! Betty was back on Broadway, all-be-it too briefly in 1980 after a 20-year absence. The 3-week stint in the musical *Annie* resulted in rave reviews. Her fans, including film critic Rex Reed, hoped that Hollywood would cast her in the part in the film version.

John Houseman and Ray Stark, both producers, to the delight of the industry, did give Betty a screen test. She took on the wild and crazy role of the mean orphanage keeper, the villainess Miss Hannigan, and she gave it her all. In the end Carol Burnett was chosen. Betty, trying to understand, said, "I guess I was a reminder of another era. They might have thought the public didn't want me anymore." She would find out otherwise.

During the run of *Annie* on Broadway, Betty taped a PBS television show called *Juke Box Saturday Night*, a program of golden oldies. But since then, she had placed show business far behind her. For at 65, we got a new Betty Hutton, complete with a college education.

As part of a tribute to composers Jay Livingston and Ray Evans at L.A. Stage Co. West in Beverly Hills, she finally made her entrance, almost at the conclusion of the two-hour program. She was greeted by a standing near-capacity crowd of 700. Overcome, she lifted teary eyes in prayer, "Thank God," while making the sign of the cross. She needed a few moments to regain her composure. "I haven't done this in a long, long time," she told the audience. "I'm a professor now!" Then she sang a number written especially for her 20 years earlier by Livingston and Evans. As an encore, she closed with "There's No Business Like Show Business." They wouldn't let her off so she told the crowd about having "a little tuck here, a little tuck there. Why shouldn't a woman look as good as she can? Men always look better - the lucky bums!" The crowd laughing, crying . . . was enthralled.

Betty was riding the Manhattan-Merry-Go-Round, but the Rocking Horse that lifted her into realms of fantasy was slowing down. She now wanted to return to the real world. She was deluged with offers to make a comeback at nightclubs, everywhere from New York to Las Vegas. "I guess I'd be, what you call, a great freak act for one time around in those clubs, but I know," she told me, "that's all. Then I'd be right back to where I was before. Nowhere!" She knew instinctively what was best for her at this time of life and moved wisely in that direction. She went home again . . . back to Portsmouth, Rhode Island.

After she bought a condo, it was school days for her now. Betty asked Fr. McGuire to help her get into Salve Regina College in Newport. "I got A's in my 2 and 1/2 years there," she boasted proudly. "There's a formal graduation ceremony in May, when I'll march along with all the kids in a robe, hat and long blue scarf hanging down my back." She earned her Master's in liberal studies and began teaching motion pictures and television at the college. She told her students, "Acting isn't what you think it is from looking at it on TV. It's a tough racket that you kids are entering." Fr. McGuire said Betty was allowed to enter college and work for her Master's degree even though she didn't have a Bachelor's degree because she was given credit for her "life experiences." He added, "Betty earned her Master's degree and is officially a member of the faculty at Salve Regina College."

Best of all, she was back with her daughters. She devoted her spare time traveling the country, telling her life story to Catholic groups and college students, emphasizing her drug addiction. "The kids of today listen to somebody who has been there, and lived to tell the tale." Afterwards, she'd throw in a few songs. "If I didn't, they'd be disappointed!" Meanwhile, she continued to write her book, *Backstage, You Can Have.* Someone I knew managed to get a hold of a few chapters in her own handwriting. My only comment: it's a disaster. She had offers from publishers and professional writers to co-author, and each time she refused. Consequently, it was never published. After hours of taping her story with me, in her own words, she only said, maybe, one day you will do it. She liked me, trusted me and opened up to me. Maybe because I am Italian, a Catholic and I liked her, too. Most of all, I may have the satisfaction of knowing I'll be helping to preserve a symbol of America's past for future generations, like a family heirloom.

Turner Classics Movies host, Robert Osborne, sensitively interviewed Betty Hutton for TCM's *Private Screenings* in April 2000; she was as boisterous as ever, pleasing her fans.

A trivia note to mention here; often people write in asking various questions about Betty Hutton and other unforgettable performers. One question was the value of a Tom Mix rocking horse, with the inscription "Tom Mix and Tony," his horse. Like Tom, Betty will also be remembered for many years to come, with movies, DVDs, CDs - and someplace within our happy memory book.

CHANGE #7-
NEW YORK PIER
AND
CHANGE #9-
EUROPE MONTAGE-TRAIN

Epilogue

The annual Communion breakfast, sponsored by the Archdi-ocese of Los Angeles for Catholics working in the entertain-ment industry, gathered together on April 1986. Many had been going to the breakfast for years, familiar faces: Penny Single-ton (from the *Blondie* series), Jon Voight, Dennis Day, to name just a few. The first recipient of the "Crux Mea Stella" (Latin for "The cross is my star") was given to Betty Hutton. A rather un-well but gallant Betty spoke about her life's experiences, rags to riches to rags and, with God's help, her rise to respectability. Her method of conquering habituation through faith in God, served as a pattern and inspiration for her students; where she taught drama in an eastern school, and who were struggling to free themselves from narcotics. And then she introduced the man who saved her, Fr. McGuire, sitting at the Dias. It was a wonderfully happy day for her. The strength she gained from that award, which she cherished more than any other accolades, would be needed in the few years she had left.

Back to teaching, however, after several years, her new

career was suddenly cut short by illness. She was diagnosed with Epstein Barr syndrome, and rather than rely upon anyone around her, she retired to Palm Springs, where she lived on Social Security and her Screen Actors Guild pension. Even those who rarely saw her were saddened by her sometimes-perfect clarity, and at others times her confusion and disorientation. Feisty Betty was fighting hard to be independent, on her own. Betty confided to a friend she had that she would rather live out her last days alone. Because of this determination she became reclusive, wouldn't answer the telephone and finally would not even answer the door, all but closing and shutting out the outside world. She was imprisoned by her own fame. When that door closed, the music stopped, the curtains came down, the lights dimmed. The metaphysical rocking horse that she rode to world fame stood still.

At sunset, on the evening of Sunday, March 11, 2007, Betty Hutton, at age 86, passed away. Around the world fans mourned for her and a reminder of their own passing years. And of the '40s and '50s, a souvenir of the times, recalling images and her music: "Arthur Murray Taught Me Dancing In A Hurry" (*The Fleet's In*, 1942), "Murder, He Says" (*Happy Go Lucky*, 1943), "His Rocking Horse Ran Away" (*And The Angels Sing*, 1945), "Doctor, Lawyer, and Indian Chief" (*The Stork Club*, 1945), and "Pappa Don't Preach to Me" (*The Perils of Pauline*, 1947). During the war, Betty went overseas to bring some hometown morale to the troops, V-mail letters, service stars that mothers hung in the front window, and, escapist movies - like hers - helped to alleviate the pain of separation.

Her life and career could well have been a Faustian pact to

win fame. Many in her profession have compromised their body and soul to win it. Betty became that rare exception - reclaiming it, before it was too late.

☆☆☆

Historians maintain that great events may tell us less about the past than the insignificant sentimental things accumulated by ordinary people, by those who loved them and could not bear to throw them away. People like George Moffatt, who lives in Berkeley who has a room dedicated to Betty Hutton memorabilia, or Edmund Arredondo, in Pasadena who is an avid Hutton collector, and Stan D'Arcy, President of The Betty Hutton Club in England, keep the memory of Betty Hutton alive. Obviously, there are countless others, like the over 300,000 Betty Hutton hits on Google. Perhaps it provided insight into what they had been like, what they endured, what their dreams had been, and which had been realized and which dashed. Betty Hutton's life helps us remember past history, but also the way we were.

Joseph Marchi, Director of the then-Canada College for The American Musical, was planning to honor Betty Hutton at an Irving Berlin Tribute. Marchi, who lives in San Mateo, California, spoke about Hutton's career to curious students at the University of London, University of St. Andrews, Scotland, and at the University Perugia in Italy. His workshops in various universities, colleges, church groups, welcomed any insight about the irrepressible Hutton. The Palace of Fine Arts, in 2008, presented a 1940s musical revue featuring "In the Mood" singers and dancers, with the String of Pearls big band performing Glenn Miller,

Tommy Dorsey, Artie Shaw, the Andrews Sisters and Betty Hutton and more with authentic arrangements, choreography and costumes.

The beat goes on to a new generation.

LaVergne, TN USA
08 February 2011
215588LV00004B/43/P

9 781593 933210